D0905063

ALL-SEASON HUNTING

ALL-SEASON HUNTING

A Guide to Early Season
Late Season
and Winter Hunting
in America

by Bob Gilsvik

WINCHESTER PRESS

Library of Congress Cataloging in Publication Data

Gilsvik, Bob.
    All season hunting.
        1. Hunting—United States.   I. Title.
SK41.G49   799.2'973   76-44533
ISBN 0-87691-181-5

Published by Winchester Press
205 East 42nd Street
New York 10017

WINCHESTER is a Trademark of Olin Corporation used
by Winchester Press, Inc., under authority and control
of the Trademark Proprietor.

Printed in the United States of America

Dedicated to my wife Pat
and our children David
and Tracy.

Acknowledgments

I wish to thank the following writers for their contributions to specific chapters:

L. James Bashline: Chapters 1, 2, 3, 4, 11; Judd Cooney: Chapters 5, 6, 7, 8, 9; William Curtis: Chapters 9, 13; Pete Czura: Chapters 2, 3, 4; Joe DeFalco: Chapters 6, 7, 8; Sam N. Fadala: Chapters 9, 12, 13, 15; Charles J. Farmer: Chapters 1, 2, 4, 11; Art Glowka: Chapters 5, 6, 7; Bob Gooch: Chapters 3, 4, 11; Norman Johnson: Chapters 9, 14; Shelia K. Link: Chapters 5, 6, 8; Frank R. Martin: Chapters 5, 6, 7, 8, 9, 10; Norman Nelson, Jr.: Chapters 5, 6, 7, 8; James R. Olt: Chapter 9; Clair F. Rees: Chapter 9; Norman Strung: Chapters 4, 8; James Tallon: Chapter 7; Russell Tinsley: Chapters 9, 13; Carlos Vinson: Chapters 1, 3, 11; Jim Zumbo: Chapters 9, 12, 13, 15.

Contents

Introduction

Are you missing half of the hunting time allotted to you? This book tells how to enjoy overlooked late-season hunting for squirrel, grouse, pheasant, and deer, as well as winter hunting for cottontails, snowshoe rabbits, jackrabbits, foxes, coyotes, and bobcats. It provides information on hunting in snow, hunting on snowshoes, cold-weather clothing, and winter camping, in addition to chapters devoted to predator calling and trapping.

It is a special time, the late season—a time of hard frosts and northern lights; a time of overcast skies and sunlit landscapes blanketed in snow; a time when you may well be the only person for miles around. The serious hunter may seek his quarry at 1,000 feet in Minnesota or 5,000 feet in Arizona. There are no geographic limitations to late-season and winter hunting in America.

ALL-SEASON HUNTING

The Opening-Day-and-Early-Season Syndrome

The planning that goes into opening day—the equipment, the oiling and the polishing of the equipment, and the talk—is awesome.

I'm as anxious as the next man to get out on opening day—despite the drawbacks: summer-green foliage, buzzing insects, crowded highways, neophyte hunters, and sometimes rather resentful landowners. Whether the hunting is good, or poor, or it rains for two days straight and I spend my time digging the car out of a mud hole, it is only one weekend of many that lie ahead. A hot meal and dry clothes, and I'm thinking about the next hunt.

If you think the hunting seasons are compacted into one or two short months each year, I suggest taking a closer look at the hunting regulations of your state or province. Consider the fascinating hunting for predators not listed. If you are really enthusiastic about hunting, there are few areas of North America that do not offer close to five months of hunting time. With opportunities available in nearby states or provinces, it adds up to a lot of hunting.

Opening day and early-season hunting offer certain advantages. It is common knowledge that after a few weeks, the local duck population wings its way south. Certainly the first couple of days of deer hunting are important. And cagey rooster pheasants get even cagier with hunting pressure. But is that the end of it?

During a typical 30-day pheasant season 50 percent of the roosters shot are shot on opening weekend. Only 5 percent of the total bag are taken during the last week. Everybody is in the field the first weekend and the kill figure is high. During the last week of the season hunters are so scarce you wonder if the season is still open.

It is a wonderful time to be afield. The birds are wary, but much of the cover is gone now and the birds are confined to smaller areas, generally areas of weeds, grasses, and swamps. Flushing a rooster is tough. But the rooster may not be alone. Roosters and hens tend to separate in the late season and flushing a whole flock of roosters is as exciting as encountering a bull moose or jumping a whitetail buck. The weather is crisp and invigorating. The landowner is taking his ease by the fire. His crops are harvested. He is more receptive to a pair of hunters who show up on his doorstep late in the season than he is to the mob that sometimes clusters there on opening day. Some of these opening-day species are downright frightening. They wear bandoliers of ammunition, sport sidearms and sabers, are death on tin cans, insulators, and highway signs. I am not sure where they originate but they rarely appear after opening day.

The ruffed grouse is surely one of the most popular game birds in North America and they are a lot easier to see and hit later in the season. When you get into the really late seasons, like the end of February closing in Ohio, Georgia, or West Virginia, or the tail end of December in New York and Minnesota, hunters are as scarce as mosquitoes and black flies. Many seem totally unaware of fantastic late-season bluebill shooting on storm-tossed lakes or the fascination of squirrel tracks in new snow. Deer hunting may be best during the first two days of the season, but the quality of the hunting is 100 percent better late in the season.

The opening-day-only zealot will probably never see a bobcat leap hissing from a snow-shrouded spruce, or a jackrabbit kick up snow as it zaps over a fence line snowdrift, nor is he likely to know the heart-hammering excitement of crawling on his stomach in the snow and deep winter silence toward a sleeping fox.

Late-season hunting is often tough hunting for game that has grown both scarce and wary. But quality hunting is high on most of our lists and quality means uncrowded hunting. You don't have to be a stoic to endure the cold, the wet, and the snow of the late seasons. All one needs are warm clothes and enthusiasm.

What is to be learned from the opening-day-early-season syndrome? Probably that it affects all of us in the same way. By early fall, every man, woman, and child who ever felt the slightest interest in hunting and the outdoors is ravenous to get out there and live out the fantasies dreamed during the off-season. For most it is a short-lived dream. For others, it lasts a little longer. Finally, there is the small but elite group that thinks hunting and the outdoors are what make life worthwhile. These hunters cry a little when the snow melts in spring. There is plenty of room in this elite group. You are probably already a member. If not, you are welcome to join us. Hunting is a fine and wholesome sport. I heartily recommend it, especially when the leaves have fallen and snow blankets the earth.

No opening-day-only-hunter, Jim Olt hunts winter crows in Kansas. (Photo courtesy James Olt)

Part One

LATE-SEASON HUNTING

ONE

Ruffed Grouse

It had snowed six inches the night before. I buttoned the collar of my wool jac-shirt. It was late-November in northern Minnesota. I was hunting an area of woodland that was too thick to tackle earlier in the season. Then I found grouse tracks in the snow, and no longer worried about discomforts. The tracks wove in and out of a dense stand of second-growth aspen. I expected a flush at any moment and from any direction. I singled out a track and attempted to follow its wanderings. The air ahead exploded with the frantic sounds of grouse flushing amid tangled branches and clutching briars. I spotted one of the grouse, fired and missed. There wasn't time for another shot. I followed the bird's line of flight, hoping to flush him again.

Thirty minutes later I wondered if I hadn't imagined the whole thing. There wasn't a trace of him or the other grouse, and there must have been at least three. Then a grouse flushed from the snow only ten feet away. I dropped him easily.

The problem was that, on landing, the birds would burrow straight into the snow and not fly again unless I was fortunate enough to walk within a few feet of them. But it had its advantages. Later that afternoon I winged a grouse, and his tracks in the snow made retrieving him an easy task.

I headed out to my car and was near the edge of the woods when two grouse erupted from the snow ahead of me. There had not been a track. These birds had roosted in the snow the night before and were sitting tight under the blanket of new snow, a condition the ruffed grouse does not mind in the least. If they cannot roost under snow they must spend the night on the surface of the snow or in a tree, where, in late winter, the temperature may be 60 degrees colder than it is under seven inches of snow. I tumbled one of the grouse as he was about to land in a spruce tree.

Commonly referred to as "partridge," the ruffed grouse ranks as the number one game bird in many states. The grouse is a plump bird 15 to 19 inches long, with rather short, rounded wings that spread from 22 to 25 inches. A prominent tail, 4½ to 7½ inches long, spreads into a broad fan. There are two color phases, the "red-tailed" and the "gray-tailed." Both phases may be found within the same areas and even within the same brood. The birds' general coloration is brown with some running toward gray or reddish.

When the first snow comes in late October or November the ruffed grouse are well prepared. They have grown furry "snowshoes" on their feet. They roost in bowls in the shallow snow or under the boughs of spruce or fir weighed down by the snow. As winter snows increase in depth ruffed grouse become more restricted in their habits, feeding largely on tree buds

and depending on the snow for warm and secure roosting cover. When the snow reaches a depth of about ten
inches most grouse roost in a snow-burrow formed by
plunging headfirst into the snow from full flight and
then "swimming" in the snow from one to several feet.

The ruffed grouse is found throughout most of Can-

Author's son, Dave Gilsvik, hefts generous limit of grouse taken by him and
his dad on late-season hunt. The shooting is easiest when the foliage is
scarce.

ada. In the United States it is found from New England to the Appalachian Mountains and throughout the upper Midwestern states and to some extent in the Northwestern states. "They are probably the most overlooked game bird in Montana," my good friend Norman Strung, an outdoor writer and guide, likes to tell visitors from the East.

The "drumming" of a male ruffed grouse, its best-known characteristic, is a part of the spring courtship to attract females from a distance. In the fall, drumming serves only to warn off other males from the area. The drumming log is a male's primary activity center. Often an activity center will be occupied 15 to 20 years before the habitat runs out. Knowledge of these activity centers and listening for fall drumming will aid in locating birds.

A lightweight 20 gauge side-by-side is the classic gun for grouse hunting. But hunters take the bird with just about any shotgun, and even pot them with rifles. For over two decades I hunted grouse with a 12-gauge pump and a shortened barrel. Including a variable-choke device, it was 25 inches long. I set the variable choke on improved cylinder. The greatest handicap to taking grouse on the wing is hunting them with full-choke bored shotguns more suited to the taking of high-flying waterfowl. Shots at grouse are very close. You need a fast opening shot pattern and plenty of shot, usually No. 7½ or No. 8 shot in low-base field or target loads. Late in the season long shots are more frequent, but you still get enough close ones to make the improved cylinder and light loads the best choice.

Ruffed grouse areas vary tremendously in population. How to maintain larger numbers of them on a more stable basis is a question that occupies game conservationists. Yet few definite answers have been found on what can be done to increase or stabilize grouse populations. The best solution found so far has been increasing second-growth stands of aspen by cutting and burning in those areas where the forest has matured beyond the point that is suitable for grouse and other forest game. Cutting or controlled burning has been beneficial not only to ruffed grouse but to deer, snowshoe rabbits, bear, and other forest game.

Hunting seems to have little effect on grouse populations. Weather may be the short-term factor in partridge populations. When partridge are scarce only persistent and experienced hunters get a few birds. Most hunters give up when their chances of success are poor.

Often a flushed grouse will fly only a short distance in a straight line, generally within 75 yards, and the persistent hunter can raise the bird again. But a grouse may stop short in the dense crown of a pine or balsam or veer sharply to one side and run after landing. Continuous searching is necessary. Two hunters are better than one. It is reasonable to think an alerted grouse will flush wild the second or third time, but often they hold even tighter. They generally head for the nearest thick cover. If none is evident a grouse may land in the open and stand motionless, exploding with rapid wingbeats at the hunter's approach.

Hunters frequently think too big. They ignore the lone grouse hangout or spots where they feel no more than two or three grouse are to be found. They opt for distant woodlands in search of better hunting. They want to find large coveys of grouse and easy hunting and to bring home impressive limits. They forget that ruffed grouse are taken one at a time.

While grouse tend to be more scattered during the late

season they nevertheless live out their lifetimes within small areas. Woodlots, or areas within larger woodlands, that were attractive to grouse early in the season will still hold birds into the late season. It just takes more hunting to find them.

Heavy underbrush with small openings is preferred by grouse, and in the case of the northwoods hunter those openings are more often than not in the form of woods trails. In the northern coniferous zones, an old woods trail carpeted with clover and wild strawberry and edged by thickets of aspen or underbrush of sumac and hazel is the most common form of ruffed grouse environment. However, as the season progresses, the hunter must pursue beyond the easy walking of woods trails.

Semi-open areas, such as moderately pastured woodlands, are ideal hunting coverts and favorites of hunters in farming areas. Pastured woodlands are invariably lush with clover. If the pasture borders on state or county land or unpastured woodland, so much the better. The pastured woodland approaches the ideal if it contains a creek, a damp alder swamp, clumps of spruce or balsam (for roosting and cover), and tall hardwood trees pocketed with stands of birch, aspen, thorn apple, and wild plum. Find the right combination and you have found a hot spot you can return to year after year. Always ask permission before hunting on private property.

Early in the season I look for grouse in moist areas. Grouse will frequently feed on succulent foods found in alder swamps. In summer they spend most of their time in moist, cool, lowland areas, feeding on the abundant plant life there; occasionally broods move onto the drier upland areas to feed on raspberries, strawberries, and blueberries.

When frosts kill off the herbaceous foods of the low-lands, the grouse move back into higher country where early fall fruits ripen, such as wild grapes, acorns, thorn apples, sumac, chokecherries, pincherries, and mountain ash berries. As fall progresses they feed on leaves of many plants including aspen, strawberry, wintergreen, clover, and bunchberry. They also learn to feed on the buds of hazel, birch, aspen, and alder.

Recent studies at the Cloquet Forest Research Center in Minnesota have indicated that grouse are highly selective in their winter food supply. Their favorite, and often exclusive, food is the flower bud of the male aspen tree. This is especially rich in oils and proteins, and is larger than other buds. Some biologists believe that many grouse will not survive especially severe winter conditions unless they have ready access to a supply of the male aspen buds. And it is also known that following an adverse winter, many birds will not be healthy enough to produce good, full hatches of chicks the next spring.

Late-season hunting becomes more difficult. Food is scarce and the birds are widely scattered. One has to head deep into the woods to find grouse. When deep snow and cold come, the birds move very little, feeding for only short periods during the day. Often they seek buds of aspen and birch in the treetops. It is possible to walk scant yards from a grouse without seeing tracks in the snow.

Evergreen thickets are worth checking out during the late season. Grouse like to roost in evergreens, and as the season progresses will spend many more hours in their roost. In deep snow, watch for snow holes on trails and in clearings. When it dive-bombs into the snow, the ruffed grouse does not want to encounter obstacles.

Highbush cranberry is a late-season treat that grouse

Distribution Range of Ruffed Grouse

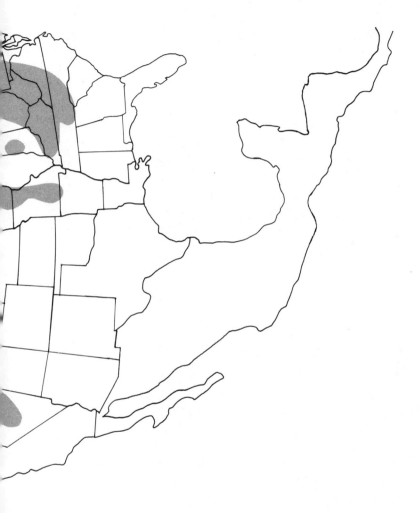

Late-season grouse like this one hang out in the heaviest available cover.

find to their liking. A Washington State hunter told me
he found grouse feeding in the comparative open of a

lowbush cranberry bog in late fall. In Wyoming, in late-season hunting, outdoor writer Charlie Farmer looks for ruffed grouse in thick alder, pine, and aspen cover along small streams.

Ruffed grouse often give away their location. Sometimes it is a nervous *prrrrt, prrrrt,* when the hunter draws near. Sometimes it is the male ruffed grouse drumming on a log, and sometimes it is the birds' footsteps in dry leaves that alerts the hunter. There is also the thunderous roar of the birds' takeoff, without which most of us would never get our gun to our shoulder in time.

What about dogs for grouse hunting? A good one will put more of everything in the gamebag. Few dogs get the hunting experience they need to develop into outstanding hunters. By all means use your dog into the late season. According to Jim Bashline, "Late-winter hunting for ruffed grouse requires a different bag of tricks than chasing them in the early fall does. The sparse cover makes the birds flush wilder and the open-choked gun that worked so well earlier becomes questionable. Longer shots are the rule, and a good, far-ranging bird dog that nails them to the ground before they hear the sound of human footsteps is a definite asset."

Early or late in the season some hunters never seem to get the hang of hitting ruffed grouse on the wing but depend entirely on potting these birds on the ground. It is a pity. Invariably the hunter uses an overly heavy, long-barreled scattergun with a full-choke barrel. Frequently grouse are flushed within five yards and the shot must be taken within 15 yards. With a lightweight scattergun and an improved cylinder or open choke, or possibly a modified setting for late-season birds, swing onto the fast departing blur, and, ignoring the leaves,

If you can't hit 'em, try a wide-open choke. Then ignore the leaves and trees—and shoot. (Photo courtesy Charles J. Farmer)

trees, and branches, pull the trigger. Often the grouse has just flown out of view as I have pulled the trigger, yet a few pellets get through the foliage and I hear the soft thud of the bird's body hitting the ground or the final thrashing of its wings as it beats its final tattoo in the autumn leaves. A fragile bird, it takes only a few pellets to bring it down.

Always get to a downed bird quickly; if it is gone, do not despair. A winged ruffed grouse will frequently stop at the nearest hint of cover. Persistent searching will leave few cripples.

I like to clean these birds on the spot. The skin is soft and one can easily puncture the stomach with one's thumb for easy removal of the viscera. This ensures good eating. Sliced and fried breast of partridge served on bread is an energizing midday meal. It takes only minutes to prepare on a Coleman stove. At home my wife, Pat, likes to quickly brown the breasts in a pan and then pop them into the pressure cooker with a half cup of water for twenty minutes. A wonderful gravy can be made by adding a can of mushroom soup to the juices.

TWO

Pheasant

Pete Czura told me "When Nebraska used to have pheasant seasons extending into mid-January, my best bet at finding the sneaky ringnecks was around plum thickets and in winter wheat patches, where the birds would group up. For fast shooting, the wheat patches offered fine opportunities if you could sneak up on the feeding birds from some tall weeds or woods fringing the wheat. Rooster pheasants leave a larger footprint in the snow, and they also make longer strides. Hens have smaller tracks and take shorter steps. Knowing this helps me pick the track I want to follow."

A mature cock pheasant will average 2¾ pounds and have a 30-inch wingspan and 35-inch length, including the long tail feathers. But few mature birds are bagged. About 75 percent of the pheasants taken annually are birds of the year. By the time hunting season rolls around most of the older pheasants have succumbed to a variety of natural causes. Hunters harvest only the surplus, because even where there's no hunting natural causes still remove 70 percent of the yearly pheasant population.

There are open seasons on pheasant in 36 states and four Canadian provinces. The pheasants natural range extends from southern Maine, Vermont, and New Hampshire, through all of Massachusetts, Rhode Island, Connecticut, Long Island, southern New York, and all of New Jersey and westward taking in slices of Pennsylvania, Ohio, Indiana, Illinois, and southern Michigan. The range of pheasant states widens at this point to take in most of Wisconsin and Minnesota, all of Iowa, North and South Dakota, Nebraska, a part of northern Arkansas, and parts of Colorado, Wyoming, and Montana.

Some pheasant seasons in Wyoming, Jackson Hole-based outdoor writer Charlie Farmer tells me, extend through December, with scarcely any pressure during late months. Look for the birds in cattails and wild rose briars. A good dog is a must. Best spot is Bighorn basin in north-central Wyoming.

West of the Rocky Mountains, pheasants are found in Utah, southern Idaho, Washington, Oregon, and California. The Canadian provinces include Alberta, Saskatchewan, the southwestern tip of Manitoba, and southern Ontario, New Brunswick, and Nova Scotia. About 12 million pheasants are harvested annually. The hottest four states are Idaho, Nebraska, Iowa, and Illinois.

The 12 gauge in pump or automatic is a favorite shotgun for pheasant hunting, but you see everything in the field from single shots and even bolt-action guns to lightweight 20-gauge doubles. A good, all-round choke setting is modified. As you get into the late season and your targets are flushing wild, a full choke is appropriate. Loads in high-base No. 5 or No. 6 shot will do the trick in the late months.

Late-season pheasant are wary. Moments like this make it all seem worthwhile. (Photo courtesy Pete Czura)

It is no secret that pheasant hunting is not what it used to be. Pheasants are farmland birds, but what is good for farming may not be good for pheasants. Agriculture can and frequently does become too intensive for the welfare of the pheasant.

Pheasants are produced in greatest numbers on the best and most fertile lands. These are the very lands in greatest demand for other uses—uses which can destroy what the pheasant needs most. The greatest problem faced by the ringneck is lack of grassy-type cover. The shift in farm-cropping practices and land reclamation has resulted in losses of grassy cover in fields, along fence lines, marsh borders, and odd corners.

In no other form of small-game hunting is a good dog so valuable as in hunting pheasant. "The big long-tailed cacklers," Jim Bashline points out, "don't like to fly under any circumstances, and cold weather keeps them even closer to the ground. A vacuum-nosed retriever is the best pheasant finder during the late bird hunts. The close-working dog puts them in the air immediately and thus avoids those half-mile chases."

Yet there is something fascinating about tackling pheasants without a dog. I particularly enjoy hunting with only one or two partners or alone.

Let's look briefly at the pheasant's early-season habits. Soon after sunrise pheasants are in the fields of corn, soybean, wheat, or sorghum. Nearly a third of the pheasant's diet is composed of grain. After an hour or two the birds retire to a nearby thicket. With considerable hunting pressure upsetting their feeding schedule, the early-morning feed may continue into the afternoon. This works to the advantage of large parties able to hunt the sprawling fields of corn and other grains. If unmolested, the birds retire to brushy thickets after a couple of hours of feeding and do not emerge again until after mid-afternoon, when they again fill their crop. They

This Nebraska hunter has a lot going for him; warm clothing, a good dog, and uncrowded hunting with tracking snow. (Photo courtesy Pete Czura)

feed until nearly dark, then seek out large marshes or other grassy areas to roost for the night.

Distribution Range of Ring-necked Pheasant

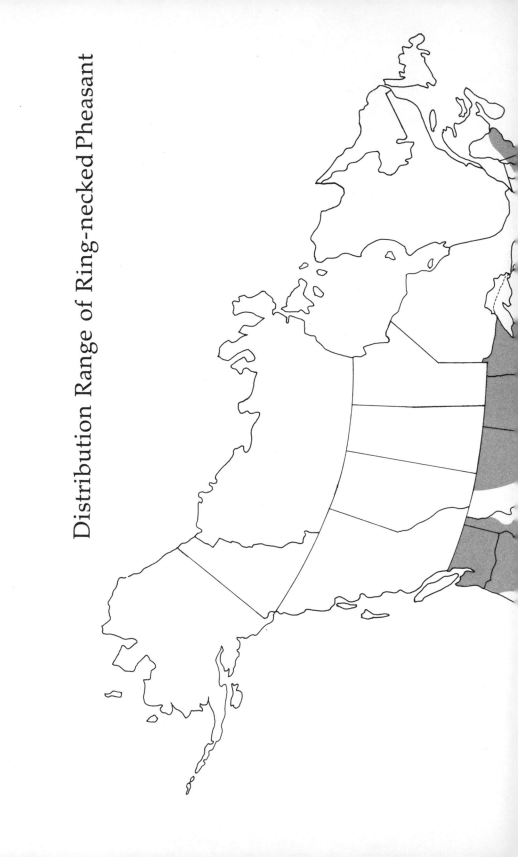

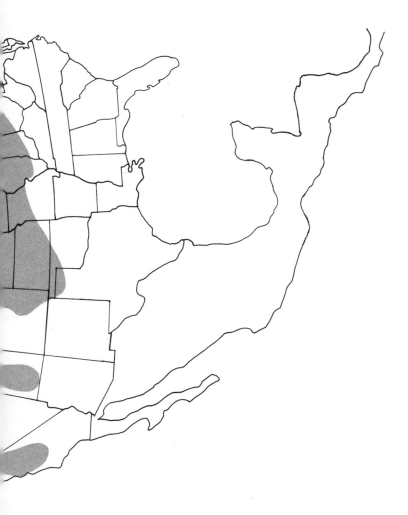

As the season progresses and crops are harvested, snow, wind, rain, and cold cause cover to deteriorate. The birds move from open fields into areas of shrubs and even small trees, where they seek acorns, weed seeds, and whatever is available. With cold weather the birds tend to start feeding later in the day. It takes a lot of energy to fight the cold, so the birds are less active. During the late season it is not unusual for pheasants to wait until about ten o'clock or, on really severe days, noontime, before feeding. This midday meal may be their sole one for the day. During storms or fresh snowfalls they may not feed at all. In the late season, most of your concentrated hunting efforts should be in swamps and marshes, especially on really nasty days.

Woodlots are overlooked by many hunters. A woodlot with acorn-bearing oak trees and scattered openings and tangled thickets is a good prospect. If it is set amid fields of harvested corn and soybeans, it is a hotspot. Frequently these woodlots contain such pheasant food as wild blackberry, grape, and sumac. Top wild foods are foxtail and ragweed. Other wild foods include lespedeza and goldenrod.

Shelter becomes increasingly important to pheasants as the season progresses. On cold, windy days look for pheasants in windbreaks such as hedgerows, fences, stone walls, gullies, creek bottoms, and swampy spots. On cold days in open Midwestern farm country, ditches are often the most likely spots. The birds stay in open fields only long enough to feed.

Walk slowly, zigzagging, or you'll walk past wily cock birds. Stop occasionally and just stand still. That will unnerve many a rooster and send him cackling into the air.

If you locate an unharvested field of corn or other

grain in the late season, it can be choice hunting. Ask permission to hunt. Bear in mind that pheasants are late risers in the cold months, so mid-morning or midday may be the best time to find them feeding. Driving works best in the late season—just follow the furrows. Pheasants are path followers and are reluctant to cross furrows. If you make a drive across a field the birds are apt to run to the left or right, but if you follow the furrows the pheasants will continue to the end of the field.

When the temperature dips to zero, pheasants tend to stay still. A fresh snow will also cause them to become immobile, at least until they get used to it. This is especially true with a snow of five or six inches. A light dusting of snow only serves to make the birds feel exposed, and they will flush wild.

A pheasant's normal flight after being flushed is 200 to 300 yards. In the head-high corn of the early season it is difficult to follow the flight of a missed bird. In the late season you can often see where the pheasant lands. You can easily pick up his trail if there is snow.

Because there is less cover in the late season, it is a good time for a single hunter or a pair of hunters to hunt pheasant. When hunting alone I like to tackle lightly pastured woodlots in good pheasant country. I like a woodlot that has scattered clumps of cover set amid oak and other mast trees. On mild days it is common for roosters to idly search the short grass in parklike openings for acorns.

Large swamp areas or grasslands seem too vast for the lone hunter to tackle. I spend a lot of time in such spots in the late season, and by narrowing my walking to key locations, find action. These key locations are islands of trees, usually aspen or sometimes clumps of high wil-

Pennsylvania pheasant hunting can be a snowy, cold affair. (Photo courtesy Jim Bashline)

lows, set amid otherwise grassy swale and cattails. These islands of trees or bushes have one thing in common: there is usually dry ground beneath them. More important, it is open ground. Rooster pheasants like to browse and scratch just like farmyard chickens. I concentrate my efforts in these islands, stopping frequently to unnerve any rooster who has run from the semi-open ground into high grass.

Do not overlook the big swamps and swales in late afternoon, when roosters begin flying in to roost. You can watch a rooster in flight and pinpoint his landing site and then walk out and flush him in exactly the same spot if he has landed in heavy grass. In dense cover the pheasant feels safe. There is no point in his running or flushing wild; in fact, you may have to almost step on him before he will flush. For this reason, do not give up on a landing site too easily. From a good vantage point you can sometimes spot two or three roosters sailing in to roost.

Another common late-in-the-day happening is for a rooster to suddenly flush from his bed only to fly for 50 yards or less and land again. Perhaps this is caused by the suspicion of an approaching predator or simply a sound. In any case, you now have him pinpointed. I can think back on numerous occasions when I had put in a full day hunting pheasant with little success only to fill my limit during the last hour of the legal shooting day.

The rooster pheasant is not a particularly difficult game bird to hit, except when their numbers are low. When the hunter puts in a full day of hunting and gets action on only one or two birds, it is easy for him to get disconcerted and miss terribly. There is a strong tendency to become so enthralled with this bird's gaudy good looks that the hunter fails to get his head down on the stock; he thus overshoots. The pheasant's length is also deceptive. Hunters who see only the colorful body and long streaming tail tend to knock off tail feathers and fail to make clean kills. Concentrate on the pheasant's head. Put the front sight of your shotgun just ahead of the pheasant's head and swing along with him for a moment, then touch off a round without stopping your swing or lifting your cheek from the stock. A good time to pull the trigger on a rising bird is just as he pauses to level off.

When he tumbles, do not waste a moment in making the retrieve. Many is the time I have seen two or three hunters fire simultaneously at a rooster who has then fallen like a ton of glue reaching for the ground. The last time this happened I was one of the hunters. We stood around for precious seconds discussing how solidly the pheasant was hit and how shot up he probably was. We never found him.

If you do not have a retriever, start running to retrieve your quarry the instant you recover from the shot. If the rooster starts running, shoot him again. Sometimes even a lightly hit rooster can be retrieved if you get to him before he has a chance to gather his wits. If I do not find a downed bird immediately, I hang my cap on the nearest bush or tuft of high grass and plunge ahead on what had been the bird's line of flight. Do not waste a moment. The rooster pheasant is one of our toughest, most tenacious game birds. It is a shame to lose one.

I like to clean these birds on the spot. The stomach lining can be torn open, even without a knife, and the entrails removed. It is shameful the way hunters will sometimes leave pheasants in a car trunk, sometimes for days, without having field dressed the birds. It is not surprising that many find wild game unappetizing. If butchers handled meat the way some unthinking sportsmen do, I would be inclined to be a vegetarian.

Pheasant is one of the top game birds for eating. My wife likes to first lightly brown the individual servings and then put them in the pressure cooker with a half cup of water for twenty minutes. For a tasty gravy, she then adds flour, water, and a teaspoon of chicken bouillon.

THREE

Squirrel

By late season, wind, rain, and snow have stripped the hardwoods of their foliage. Squirrels can spot the hunter from a distance, and stalking within shooting range is a real sport and a test of woodsmanship.

Squirrels are normally early risers, but in the winter months they sleep late, and will feed into the late-morning hours. They don't like raw, windy days. Cold temperatures alone will not keep them holed up, and a crisp sunny day will see them out and about at high noon absorbing some sunshine.

The two most popular squirrels are the gray and the fox squirrel. The eastern gray squirrel is from 15 to 20 inches long—seven to ten inches of that length being a bushy tail. The western gray squirrel is a little larger. Both are predominately gray in color with their tails lightly bordered with white-tipped hairs. The eastern gray squirrel is found all across the eastern United States. The western gray squirrel is found only in a narrow strip along the Pacific coast.

Jim Zumbo uses a rock for natural blind as he waits to waylay bushytail in late winter. (Photo courtesy Jim Zumbo)

Fox squirrels are found across most of the same range as the eastern gray squirrel, but not as far north. Their range extends farther west of the Mississippi than does the gray.

The .22 rimfire rifle is the best choice for squirrel hunting among many hunters. In areas of the South, where vegetation is so thick that any glimpse of a squirrel is a brief one, hunters prefer shotguns. Shotguns in 20 gauge are the most popular for squirrel, usually with loads of No. 6 shot. For the rifleman, .22 Long Rifle ammunition is the favorite. Hollow-point ammo makes too devastating a wound.

I asked Pete Czura about squirrel hunting in Nebraska. "Nebraska squirrels aren't exactly patsies," he replied. "Generally, if we have a good mast year, there is food everywhere, and to an experienced hunter that means squirrels are everywhere and not concentrated around a few good food trees. Best squirrel hunting comes after a rain or snowfall, when stalking becomes easier because the dampened leaves won't crackle like rifle shots signaling your approach to an alert squirrel."

Wear subdued, drab-colored clothing when you hunt squirrel. After a snowfall, wear white. Does this sound like a bit much for the lowly squirrel? Nothing is too much when it comes to outfoxing either the gray or the fox squirrel. Anything unusual sends them into hiding.

When you and your hunting partner have a squirrel up a tree it is best to take turns shooting. The best bet is for the shooter to assume a comfortable shooting position and watch for the squirrel while his partner circles the opposite side of the tree.

When hunting alone and you have a squirrel treed, pick up a dead limb and then crouch in a spot where you

It takes skill to score on a squirrel on the ground with a .22 rimfire.

have a good view of many branches. Sit quiet for a spell. Then throw the dead limb over to the opposite side of the tree. You will get your shot when the squirrel scrambles over to your side of the tree.

Another trick for the lone hunter is to tie a string to a bush, then walk to the opposite side of the tree. Sit quietly for a few minutes. Then shake the bush with the string. This works surprisingly well, but shoot quickly—the squirrel will not stay fooled for long. When all else fails, it sometimes pays to stand right up against the tree trunk and, while looking up into the branches, move slowly around the trunk.

Look for the fuzzy outline of the squirrel's tail. Watch for any form on the side of tree limb or trunk. A scope sight comes in handy for taking a closer look at a suspicious form amid shaded branches. If you have never used a scope sight for deer or other big game and are anxious to try, a good way to get used to one is to have one mounted on your .22 rifle. In fact, it is a good idea to use the rather large scope size normally used on big-game rifles. These are far superior to scopes designed expressly for the .22s. Their large size gives them abundant light-gathering power which makes them ideal for spotting squirrels in shadowed branches. When you get the hang of popping squirrels off tree limbs with head shots, bowling over a deer or moose will seem like easy pickings.

What do squirrels eat in winter? Tennessee-based Carlos Vinson tells me that they feed mostly on acorns and beech mast during winter.

I have found that an unpicked field of corn is a tempting target for squirrels. The fox squirrel is especially daring when it comes to running long distances from the nearest tree. Fields of picked corn, if left unplowed, are also good late-season hot spots. Squirrels will dig through snow to reach the corn missed by the picker.

The squirrel's diet consists of many things, including nuts, fruits, berries, buds, seeds, twigs, and flowers. One squirrel will consume as much as 100 pounds of food a year and will spend much of his time gathering it. They are noisy about it. They variously grunt, purr, chatter, and even growl. The patter of nut shells falling to the ground and picked up by a sharp-eared hunter has cost many a squirrel his life. Even the scuttling sounds of squirrels climbing trees or running through dry leaves can tip off the alert hunter.

The hunter must be cautious, too. Use the method employed by deer hunters. Take a few steps, stop and listen for five minutes, then take a few more steps and

Distribution Range of Gray Squirrel

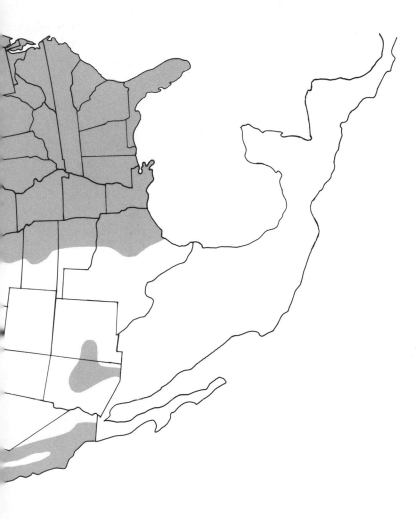

repeat. When a squirrel is spotted it frequently pays to rush the animal. If sufficiently alarmed, the squirrel will dash up the nearest tree rather than select one with a den hole. A squirrel is pretty safe once he dives into a hole, but you can still get him by concealing yourself nearby or simply sitting quiet in full view and waiting. If he doesn't poke his head out within 20 minutes, it is best to move on. Your time was not wasted. While you were sitting, it gave other alerted squirrels in the woods a chance to calm down and resume their normal activities.

Few of us are able to confine our hunting to times when conditions are perfect for the quarry. Usually we have a weekend or vacation day in which to hunt, and if we want to hunt we go out no matter what the conditions. But I'll turn down a squirrel hunt if a very strong wind is blowing or is forecast. Squirrels are reluctant to feed on the ground on windy days. A strong wind can muffle the approach of a predator, animal or man. On windy days, they feed almost entirely in the tree tops.

If you find yourself in a position where it is hunt in the wind or not at all, and you have a partner, there is still hope for bagging a few bushytails (I'm presuming that the wind is not a bitterly cold arctic blast). Work as a team. Move through the woods parallel with each other and about 30 yards apart. As you walk, concentrate on the tree limbs between you. Watch for movement. Squirrels will scuttle from one side of a tree trunk or limb to another to avoid exposing themselves to one or the other hunter. This movement helps you to spot him. It is not easy. But it will work.

Squirrels are almost always active in early fall, either on the ground or in the tree tops. In the winter it is a different story. You can have wonderful hunting one

Hunter uses large rock for rest as he takes aim at squirrel. (Photo courtesy Jim Zumbo)

day and get skunked the next. In the winter, barometric pressures or other mysterious forces probably have something to do with how active squirrels are. One clue is to note if squirrels in your yard or nearby city park are active. If they seem very active and plentiful, it can pay to get in your car and head for your favorite squirrel woods.

If you are hunting in snow, and conditions are such that squirrels are not active, you can still make use of your time observing their tracks and trails. Take note of any obvious den trees. The next time you hunt you can approach these activity centers with extra caution. Watch, too, for squirrels feeding in nearby cornfields. I remember one winter's day when I saw seven gray squirrels scramble out of a picked cornfield and every one ran up the same tree by the woods' edge. The squirrel season was open but I was toting my .243 and hunting foxes.

A good squirrel dog will improve your hunting 100 percent. Almost any kind of dog will sight-chase squirrel. A dog will force the squirrel to run up the first tree it comes to, something the less agile hunter cannot copy. With some encouragement, almost any kind of dog will learn to trail squirrels by scent. However, some of the best squirrel dogs are in the rat terrier and fox terrier class. On several occasions, while hunting squirrels, I have been joined by farm dogs who seemed to know exactly what I was up to and who immediately began treeing squirrels for me. One was a German shepherd and another a black Labrador.

When hunting early in the season, remain in one spot and wait for the game to show itself. Then take a shot from where you are, or attempt to approach to within closer range. In cold weather this gets uncomfortable. On a sunny winter's day it can be worth trying if squirrels are very active. A good location would be along a fence line or narrow lane separating unharvested corn and woods.

Do not overlook the use of binoculars in late-season squirrel hunting. They are useful for scanning small clumps of trees that are far out in open, snow-shrouded fields. Fox squirrels are very much at home in such isolated habitat, and they stand out clearly against a snowy background. I have often sighted fox squirrels while glassing for red fox.

To score on squirrels with head shots only, your rifle must be accurately sighted-in. Use a bench rest, or put padding over your car hood and use that. Do not make the mistake of taking random shots at a knothole or match cover. Do it right. Take the time to color a one-inch bull's-eye on a sheet of white paper, or use a commercial target. Pin this to the side of a cardboard box and set against a safe backstop. Old gravel pits are good locations for zeroing your rifle. Most squirrel hunters like to zero their .22 rimfires to hit point of aim at 20 yards. Do not be satisfied until you are accurately sighted-in. Choose a warm day and bring lots of ammo. A little extra time spent adjusting your scope, receiver, or open sights will save you a lot of frustration later when trying to connect with half an inch of squirrel head showing above a tree limb. Adjustments for elevation and windage are clearly marked on scope and receiver sights. With open sights, elevation is adjusted by raising or lowering the rear sight. Windage, left and right, is attained by tapping the front sight to the left or right. If a three-shot group is hitting high and to the left, move the rear sight down and the front sight to the right.

One of the toughest feats of woodsmanship and marksmanship is to score on a squirrel with a .22 rifle while the squirrel is on the ground and unaware of your presence. This is especially difficult for the hunter on the move. It is difficult to get close to jittery squirrels. Even then, the shot will probably be a long one. Knowledgeable hunters know exactly what their rifle can do at various ranges and take squirrels out to 60 yards. The man with a .22 rimfire Magnum can extend that range to 90 or 100 yards. It is not easy, even with a scoped rifle. Most .22s are lightweight, and getting off a steady shot under field conditions is difficult. Take advantage of natural rests, old stumps, logs, hummocks of ground, or whatever.

The .22 Magnum provides flat shooting at long range. Here is how my scoped Winchester Model 9422 Magnum hits when sighted-in at 20 yards with Winchester-Western Super-X 40 grain Magnum rimfire full metal case loads:

5	yds:	¾ inch low
10	yds:	½ inch low
20	yds:	bull's-eye
40	yds:	¼ inch high
50	yds:	⅝ inch high
75	yds:	bull's-eye
100	yds:	1¾ inches low

Soak squirrels overnight in a water and salt solution. Generally, I like to cut squirrels into serving-size pieces, simmer for an hour or so, and then brown. But here is a recipe that is a little different and utilizes the squirrel all in one piece:

Dressed squirrels, about 3
½ cup vegetable oil
3 tablespoons lemon juice

2 cups bread crumb
   dressing
salt
pepper
½ stick butter
1 tablespoon grated
   onion

Wash the cleaned squirrels under running water and wipe dry with a clean cloth. Mix the oil and lemon juice, pour over the meat and let stand one hour. Stuff the squirrels with a good bread dressing, salt and pepper them, and roast in a 350-degree oven two hours. Baste frequently with butter to which a little grated onion has been added.

FOUR

Deer

Most hunters choose the earlier days of the season to deer hunt. Late-season deer hunting holds no guarantees, except that you will enjoy uncrowded, quality hunting.

Late-season hunting for mule deer is excellent if you are seeking a trophy buck. In the mountain states, deep snows will drive the big bucks down to lower elevations. Norman Strung, outdoor writer and guide, who lives near Bozeman, Montana, tells me it is not uncommon to get four feet of snowpack at 8,000 feet. Snows of such depth will drive mule deer to the lowlands.

As the season winds down in Virginia, Bob Gooch reports, antlerless hunting prevails throughout most of the state, giving hunters who have not yet scored an opportunity to put venison in their freezer.

The deer is the number-one big-game animal in the United States and a challenge to hunters everywhere. The whitetail and mule deer appear similar at a glance, but a closeup look reveals the larger ears of the mule deer and a black-tipped tail. The antlers of the mule deer tend to be higher and they are branched. The main beam is evenly divided at the first fork. Each branch then divides again.

The whitetail has a tail that is brown on top and white underneath. The whitetail has the largest tail of any deer in America. It is hard to miss when he runs because he flashes the white underside like a flag, a signaling device to warn other deer of danger. In the bucks, the antler tines are unbranched and extend upward from the main beam.

The black-tailed deer of the Pacific coast (considered one of the muleys) has a tail that is black on top from tip to base. There are many subspecies of the whitetail. These generally tend to be smaller deer as you get into the southern, more temperate zones.

The range of the whitetail is extensive. It covers all of the eastern United States and the southern parts of the Canadian provinces bordering on the United States, and extends into the Rocky Mountain states and Mexico. They are even found in pockets along the Pacific coast.

Mule deer are confined to the western states, Mexico, northwestern Canada, and Alaska.

There was a time when the choice of rifle for deer hunting was confined to a half-dozen calibers and models. The lever action .30-30 and the bolt action .30-06 ranked high in popularity. Today the choice of calibers and models would confuse anyone. Still, the .30-30 and .35 Remington are popular calibers in lever-action carbines as eastern brush guns for whitetails. The .30-06 and .270 Winchester are popular calibers in bolt-action rifles for long-range shots at mule deer. It is not uncommon, however, to find the long-range models in the hands of eastern hunters and the close-range models in the hands of western hunters.

Late in the season deer become more nocturnal. Be on a morning stand before daylight. In the afternoon, stay as late as the law allows. (Photo courtesy Charles J. Farmer)

I think it depends a great deal on the type of hunting you do. I hunt whitetails in heavy brush, but much of my hunting is trail watching, if there is no snow, and I use a scope-sighted Winchester Model 70 in .243. This was my choice for an all-around rifle that I could use for varmint hunting, too. I use this same rifle for crows, jackrabbits, and foxes. It feels comfortable in my hands and with it I am able to pick up openings in the brush to score on whitetails.

If I lived in one of the western states, I would be more inclined to own a .270 as an all-around caliber. This would retain more zap at longer ranges and be a better choice for heavier big game.

Bullet placement is still the all-important consideration in deer hunting. Any of the popular calibers will do the job when placed in a deer's boiler room. Breaking a deer's leg with an elephant gun would be no more effective than doing the same thing with a .30-30. If you like to pussy-foot through the woods and take your chances with running shots, a light carbine is a good choice. They provide fast gun handling. If most of your hunting is done from a stand or across canyonlands, you can take your choice from a selection of heavier, but extremely accurate, bolt-action rifles. I've had good success with my .243, but if I were to select a caliber strictly for deer hunting, I would go to a heavier load. I think it wise to use enough gun for the quarry sought. Heavier loads leave a good blood trail. This becomes all-important when a hit is made a little too far back from the chest cavity.

In lever-action carbines, some popular calibers include .30-30 Winchester, .35 Remington, .358 Winchester, .444 Marlin, and .44 Remington. In bolt-action rifles, popular calibers include .243 Winchester, .270 Winchester, 7mm Remington Magnum, .30-06 Springfield, and .308 Winchester. Don't go into a funk if I failed to mention the caliber you own. Remember, it's where you hit 'em that counts.

Open, parklike woods are nice to walk through but they make poor habitat for deer, especially whitetails. Old forests tend to get this way as the trees mature. Cutting and fire are two fast routes to increasing lush second-growth, the condition most favored by deer. Ideal is the woodland that contains a mixture of trees and underbrush in various stages of growth, and where planned cutting is employed to remove trees as they mature. We have a tendency to pat ourselves on the back because of our prolific deer herds, yet this condition will not last forever without planned cutting and other wildlife management practices.

Recent pulp or logging operations are a big attraction to deer. They will move in while work is still in progress. Felled trees mean tender branch tips within easy reach. Even rabbits and grouse move in to feed. Hunters will do well to seek such locations when selecting a new hunting area. By the late season, hunting pressure will likely force deer to temporarily abandon such feeding sites if close to the roadside. Deer, particularly the whitetail, do not go far, however.

Familiarity with the area is essential. If you have not hunted in the selected location before, by all means get in preseason scouting time. Obtain maps of the area. A topographic map is helpful in locating swamps and other low-lying areas where hunting pressure will have driven the whitetail. Whitetails will seek such sheltered locations after only four or five days of hunting pressure. A narrow opening in a cedar swamp can be a hotspot for early and late in the day posting. Deer become more nocturnal than usual by the late seasons.

If you plan to do any standing, it is imperative you be

Western hunters who want trophy bucks wait for the late season and snow in the high country. The result is pictured above. (Photo courtesy Norman Strung)

in the woods while it is still dark. The last hour of the day should be spent just off an obvious deer run that is also near a trail that you can follow to camp in the dark. A wise precaution when walking in darkness in the deer woods is to carry a small flashlight. It would not do to be mistaken for a deer.

Deer are alarmed by unusual sound, sudden movement, and scent. Steady, quiet walking may not spook them. But sudden movement in a fixed stand will be noticed immediately, as well as your scent. When moving or located on stand, always keep wind currents or air movement at your face. When there is no noticeable wind, always work against thermal currents which move from low to high ground during the daytime when temperatures are warming and reverse direction when the temperature is declining from dusk to dawn. I remember the direction of thermal currents by picturing two mule deer I shot from the same rockslide in Montana. I was above the buck I shot in the morning and below the buck I shot in the afternoon.

Always look for deer sign in a given section. Snow, of course, is always helpful. In its absence, however, there should still be visible signs of buck rubs, droppings, scrapes, and defined runs.

"In spite of the thrills of just being out on opening day," said Jim Bashline, "I have become a late-season hunter here in Pennsylvania whenever possible. The competition from other hunters is less and an individual deer track is easier to follow. It may be mere coincidence, but the biggest trophy bucks are usually taken by the lone hunter who just happens to be in that fabled 'right place at the right time'. That combination of events seldom takes place on opening day."

I asked Charlie Farmer about deer hunting in the cowboy state. "Most deer seasons in Wyoming end by November," he said, "before heavy snowfall in the state. But there are a few, good late-season prospects,

Successful deer hunting depends on finding the greatest concentration of deer in any area. Look for sign, tracks, trails, rubs, and scrapes.

especially in the northeast corner of the state, in the Black Hills. Good bet for hunting whitetails is hunting from mid-November to December 7, when the season ends. Bucks are in the middle of rut then and there should be plenty of good tracking snow. Most seasons on mulies end too early in the state to qualify as late-season sport, to the dismay of many hunters who see countless good bucks along the road in late November and December."

"When the deer season opens in Nebraska," said Pete Czura, "I dream of snow and bad weather. It seems when nasty weather occurs I score more often, particularly if I hunt in the rugged butte country of Nebraska's Pine Ridge [northwest corner of the state] where tracking deer in the canyons is certain to lead a hunter to his prey. If the weather is fair, I don't look for deer. Instead, I hunt for places that have a good deer food supply, such as acorns, wild rose, wild plum, and chokecherry, then wait for one that is bound to come along."

Snow is doubly important in late-season deer hunting. Deer tend to move at certain times, lie low during others. These movements become more difficult to fathom in the late season. I think that standing is an effective way to take deer early in the season but not nearly as effective during the late season. For one thing, cold weather of 10 to 15 degrees below zero, as I experienced on a recent late-season hunt, makes standing difficult. For another, there are fewer hunters in the woods to move deer and the deer are less inclined to move on their own, except in the case of mountain mule deer, which can develop a sudden urge to migrate.

As winter approaches, George Mattis told me, the whitetail learns to conserve his energy for the bare essentials necessary for his existence. He now roams a lesser area, and the hunter must adjust to this change in the behavior of his quarry. Standing, however, can pay off if two or more hunters work together. For example, one or more hunters remain on a trail watching likely crossings while one or more hunters work the brush

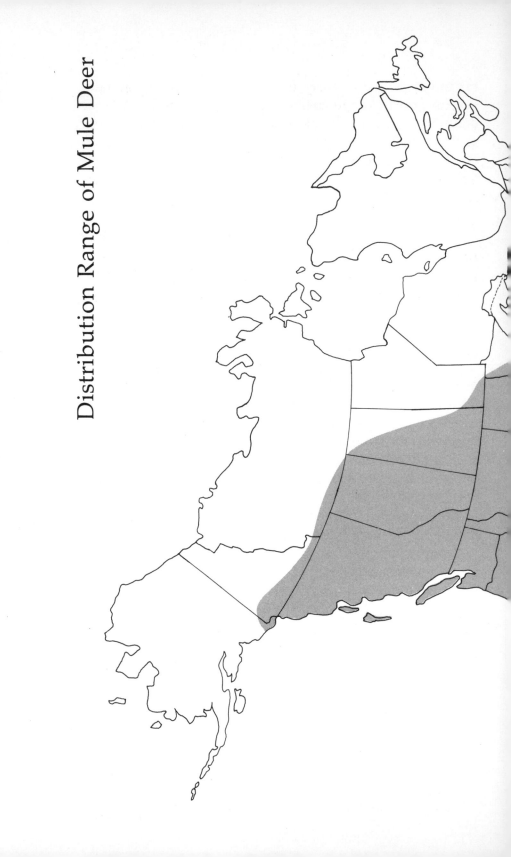

Distribution Range of Mule Deer

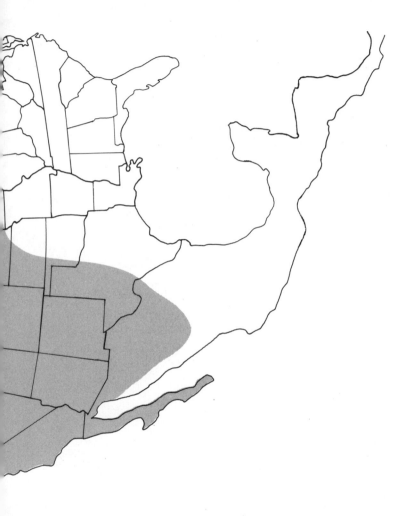

57

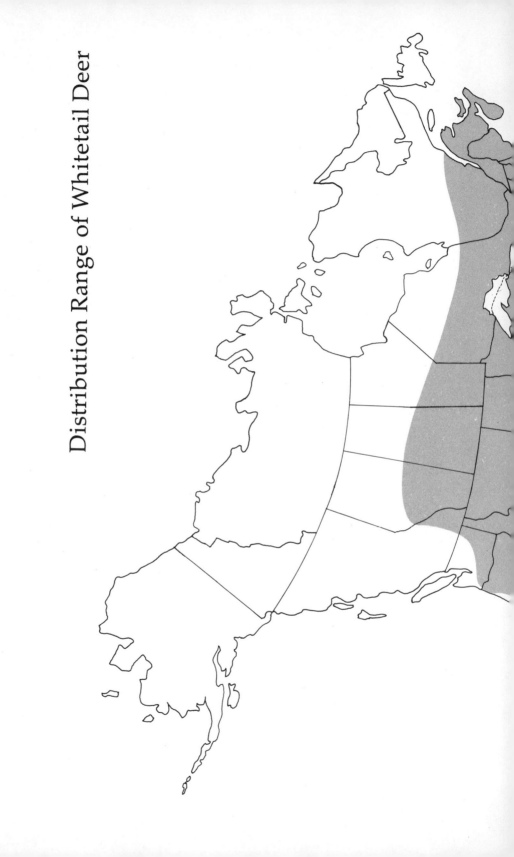

Distribution Range of Whitetail Deer

within the general area. Nothing is more disconcerting than to follow the tracks of a big buck and find where it has crossed open lanes and clearings where a partner could have had an easy shot.

On a recent whitetail deer hunt I found where my partner, Dennis Seline, was following the track of a huge buck. I could not resist following their tracks on the chance of getting in on the action. I was aghast to find that the buck had crossed several openings where I had spent brief periods earlier that morning.

I used to think that tracking deer in snow was a lost art, but Dennis Seline does so regularly with good success. He does equally well without snow. His secret? He devotes much time and effort to locating an area with plentiful deer signs. He advises to get into an area with plenty of deer and your chances will rise dramatically. Many hunters fail to do this; instead they spend days hunting a favorite deer area with little deer sign when only a quarter mile away the woods may be crawling with deer activity.

Tracking deer is difficult if the snow cover is old. Where there is a concentration of deer, old snow will be riddled with tracks. One way to determine an old track is by pushing your fingers into the track. If the edges are frozen, you are on an old track. Take the time to feel the texture of the snow in the track of a deer you know has been recently flushed from its bed. New tracks are evident in old snow if there is a sudden thaw.

Many hunters believe they are not good enough to track deer in snow. In fact, it can be done by relatively inexperienced hunters. Start by dressing lightly. You can do so in even cold weather because you will be on the move. Your outer clothing should be of wool. Goosedown is light and warm but the outer material of coats and jackets is made of synthetic material that is noisy. A good compromise is a goosedown vest under a wool shirt or jac-shirt (wool coats are too heavy). Boots should be of rubber or otherwise waterproof. For more details, see Chapter Seven on cold-weather clothing. Your rifle should be one you are familiar with and can shoot fast and accurately.

When you jump a whitetail in woods cover the average time to get off a shot is about three seconds. You might have more time with a mule deer in open terrain, but don't count on it. By moving as quietly as you can without dawdling, you can quickly follow a deer to its daytime bedding site. Avoid rambling tracks left by feeding deer. Follow tracks that appear to have a definite destination. What hunters do not realize is that deer commonly remain in bed under a spruce tree or windfall and let them walk by. By sticking to its track, you will force the deer to flush. You may get within 40 yards of the deer before he makes his move—sometimes a lot closer.

If you miss a good opportunity at a jumped deer, it may be your last, particularly if you are trailing a large buck. So the next step is to try and anticipate his route and head him off. Deer will circle, as well as stop to browse, even when being trailed. By anticipating the next move you can score. For example, if you have been trailing a buck south, into the wind, and then he abruptly heads to the west and crosses a logging trail, one possible move is to jog for up to a quarter-mile south down the logging trail and stop at a likely crossing. There is a chance the buck will cut back across the logging trail to resume his route south on basically the same line he was traveling before.

Wait for twenty or thirty minutes. If nothing shows,

head back down the trail the way you came, to see if the buck crossed sooner than you figured. If he did, and there are still a few hours of daylight, get back on his trail and watch for another opportunity. Needless to say, you also want to watch for the buck up ahead. A perfectly motionless deer, even in snow, is easy to miss. Don't be discouraged by failure. Your next attempt may be successful.

Such trailing can get you off the beaten path in a hurry. With a compass and map of the area you can travel worry-free. But give yourself plenty of time to get out of the woods before dark.

You can get shots at deer by simply moving very slowly through an area that shows plenty of deer sign, tracks, trails, droppings, scrapes, rubs, and beds. With this kind of hunting it is impossible to walk too slowly. About 90 percent of your time should be spent peering and listening. If you cover more than 1½ miles in a day's time, you are moving too fast. Study the cover in all directions. Squat down on your heels and look under the brush. Watch your backtrail. A deer may freeze and let you pass and then cross behind you. It takes determination and discipline to keep this up all day. It gets easier once you learn how effective it is.

If you occasionally snap a twig or stumble, do not give up or revert to moving fast and noisily through the brush. Even deer make sounds now and then. You will alert a deer with a snapped twig but he will hold tight until he can identify you by sight or smell.

The hunter who stands and watches a clearing can expect to see a whole deer. Not so the stalker. Look for parts of deer: an ear, an eye, a leg, a part of an antler, a patch of hide. Small, lightweight binoculars will help

Float hunting for deer, as in this Sportspal canoe, can be profitable. Game won't pay much attention to objects on the water. (Photo courtesy Jim Bashline)

you to identify suspicious objects in shadowed cover.

Listen for sounds: leaves rustling, branches popping, rocks clinking, water splashing, the thud of hooves on frozen ground. I once heard a fine whitetail approach in crusted snow. My hearing is poor, but the deer made more noise than the average hunter.

Where I hunt deer in northern Minnesota, the best time to catch bucks in the rut is the first ten days in November. Yet during the last week in November it is common to find places where bucks have opened up scrapes in the snow. Even a few does are still receptive. The scrapes worth watching are those close to heavy cover.

Keep abreast of the weather. Just before and immediately after a snowstorm, deer will be up and about feeding all day. Hunting during a snowstorm can be uncomfortable, but few times are better suited for silent stalking. If you are in a cedar swamp or other heavy cover where much deer sign has been noted, you have a good chance of encountering action. A lot of hunters will stay in camp during bad weather. For the serious deer hunter, it is an excellent time to be out.

When selecting a stand location, remember that deer are reluctant to cross open areas after there is a snow cover. Select either a very narrow opening or an area interspersed with cover. Far better to have to make a difficult shot in cover than to get no action in a clearing.

In summary, select a hunting area where recent pulp cutting or logging has occurred or where deer food is otherwise plentiful. The lush second-growth from cutting or fire will keep deer in the area for many years. Remember that deer are smart enough to move away from the heaviest hunting pressure. You can turn this to your advantage by working those deeper areas toward which they are likely to be driven. Any standing (posting) you do for deer that are not being pushed by your partner or other hunters should be done very early and very late in the day as deer grow more nocturnal with hunting pressure.

Deer senses are superior to human senses, but human intelligence can reduce this superiority. This means that the hunter must have knowledge of the area and of deer habits, ability to recognize signs of deer presence and movement, a preconceived plan of action, and, above all, hard work. A lot of hunters want to *shoot* a deer, but they forget that it's the *hunting* that makes the sport.

I am convinced that a low-power scope sight will reduce misses on deer, even those shots in brush where you have three seconds to score. There is less tendency to shoot at the whole animal with a scope sight. Scope sights are fast—faster than open sights. With open sights one must not only align the front sight on the deer but must align it with the rear sight as well. With a scope sight you simply plant the cross hairs in the center of the deer's chest, and squeeze the trigger. But don't make the mistake of traipsing into the deer woods with a scope sight you have never used. If you cannot utilize it for varmint shooting or other off-season practice, at least put in some time shooting at paper targets over and above the required sighting-in before a hunt. Once you get used to a scope sight you will feel handicapped without one. I'm sure there would be fewer hunters mistaken for deer if everyone used a scope sight. A scope sight is just the thing for low-light conditions.

A great argument among hunters is where to shoot a deer. I'll take a neck or head shot, but only if that is the only shot offered. Many feel that a neck or head shot means a clean kill or a clean miss. Unfortunately, this is not always true. Deer will run for miles with the jaw or the whole front of the face shot away. Not a pretty sight. A neck shot is not fatal unless the spine is damaged or a main artery severed. It is my experience that the best place to hold your sights is in the center of the deer's chest cavity. If you hit a little too high you will drop the deer instantly with a spinal shot; a little low and you hit the heart. Deer seldom travel over 50 feet when hit square in the lungs.

Always check for signs of a hit when you shoot at deer. No animal is more tenacious of life. A well-hit deer will more often than not run like mad. If the deer has been hit in the heart or lungs, he is running dead. You will find him shortly. If a deer has been lightly grazed, you can follow him for miles and never catch up with him. When you wing a deer you have the responsibility to finish the job if at all possible.

I don't waste a moment field dressing my deer. Then I prop the deer's chest onto a log with the open stomach cavity facing down and the hind legs spread apart. I prefer to leave the deer like this for a couple of hours before dragging him out. This gives the animal a chance to cool. If you have to leave the deer overnight, he will keep well in this position.

I butcher my own deer. I debone most cuts and remove every trace of tallow. When I flesh away meat for deerburger, I am fussy about allowing any tallow in these scraps. You are bound to have some, but I make every effort avoid it. When I have this meat ground I do not have pork or other meat added. I like venison the way it is.

Cook venison at moderate temperature. Don't make the mistake of trying to kill the deer twice by overcooking. If you like meat a little rare, there is no reason not to prepare venison this way. By all means, try barbecueing venison. Oh! but it's good.

Part Two

THE SECOND SEASON

FIVE

Hunting in Snow

The success or failure of hunting in snow is directly proportional to your comfort, which means you have to have the proper clothing and footwear as well as know how to hunt in the snow. Also, you must be up to the physical demands of tramping through the frozen country.

Water repellent outer garments can be purchased easily, but better physical conditioning is hard for most of us to maintain on a year-round basis. Fortunately, it is not too painful to get back into shape if you do not allow yourself to get too far gone. A friend of mine recently hunted successfully for elk and deer in Montana. He and his companions hunted in knee-deep snow at elevations of 8,000 to 10,000 feet. My friend is lean and hard and one of the most active individuals I know. Still, he was not satisfied. He spent six weeks prior to the trip conditioning himself. The first two days of his hunt were nevertheless grueling, he told me. After that he felt fine. Other members of the party had a very difficult time.

It's a whole new ball game when you hunt in snow.

You have an advantage if you live where winter game is close to home. You can get out often. Each time out increases energy and staying power. You get an abundance of health and muscles without really trying. Do not, however, use your increased energy to drive a hunting partner into the ground. On the other hand it is not wise to try to keep pace with someone who is in better shape than you.

Make a point of pacing yourself. It is easy to start breezing along on foot or snowshoes when you are feeling good. It is also easy to perspire freely and not notice it, and this catches up with you when you slow down or remain motionless. Pace yourself and you can hunt all day in snow. You will also be better prepared to shoot accurately when the chance comes, and to think more clearly when a fast decision is needed.

Keeping dry is important. Dry feet are of primary concern. Rubber footwear, Art Glowka, a Connecticut outdoor writer tells me, is essential. A clean pair of wool socks with some percentage of nylon (for strength) is a good way to start the day. Felt soles or liners will help keep rubber footwear warm. These must be dried out nightly. If you leave a pair of sorrel boots out on a cold porch overnight with perspiration-soaked liners, the liners will freeze to the soles of the boots. The Air Force "bunny boot" is very warm when worn with two felt inner soles. They are very slippery on hard-packed snow, but excellent when worn with snowshoes.

You can enjoy dry, warm feet by simply wearing a roomy pair of overshoes over comfortable workshoes. But first pull a pair of heavy wool-synthetic socks over the outside of the workshoes. Then put on the overshoes. When hunting in snow of any depth, always use twine to tie your trouser legs snugly around your boot or overshoe tops. This will keep snow out of your boot tops. Commercial gaiters and anklets are availiable.

Clothing will be discussed more thoroughly in Chapter Seven, so for now let me say that when hunting in snow, especially snow that is the least bit wet, it is hard to beat wool. Wool pants are vital.

The more one hunts in snow the more enthused and expert one gets at track identification, and where you find the track is important. I doubt I would notice a fox track in town. I would assume it to be the track of a dog, if I noticed it at all. On the other hand, if I saw a single-file track following a fence line in farmland terrain, I would presume it was the track of a red fox. It could be a dog track, but dog tracks show a lot of pad and rarely appear far from the road or farm. By following the track for any distance, I can learn what the animal is up to, and this helps me name it.

I think most outdoorsmen can make pretty fair track identification in areas where they have hunted a lot. For the last couple of winters I have been doing a lot of winter hunting in an area where bobcat and the weasel-like fisher are common. I might not have recognized either track in my old stomping grounds. Now I spot them instantly, and am becoming a fair judge of the size of the cats. Most animals reach almost adult size by their first winter. Bobcat will vary considerably in size.

Determining the freshness of tracks can be very critical. If you are hunting bobcat with hounds, don't release the hounds unless the cat track is very fresh. To set them loose on an old track will mean many hours of cold tracking. If the track is too old there will not be any scent. The track itself means little to the dog.

A concentration of fresh deer tracks within a small area indicates a good place to concentrate your deer hunting efforts. However, if the tracks are not fresh, the deer may now be half a mile distant. A big aid in determining the freshness of tracks is knowing the time of the last snowfall, as even a light dusting of snow is critical.

There comes a time when you should get your nose

Adequate clothing is needed when you hunt in snow. These men are well prepared. (Photo courtesy Norm Nelson)

out of the track and start looking for the quarry. Tracks can tell you if an area contains game, but unless you are actually trailing an individual animal, it pays to be looking well ahead for the deer or rabbit. Studying an animal's track while he is slipping over a distant hillside is not going to put him on the meatpole.

Know the effect snow has on game birds and animals. When snow has a depth of 10 inches or more, most ruffed grouse roost in a snow burrow, formed by plunging headfirst into the snow from full flight and then by "swimming" in the snow for one or several feet. Formation of hard crusts on the surface of the snow is one of the important hazards ruffed grouse face. On the surface of the snow, the grouse not only use up energy at a high rate to keep warm, but they are also more likely to become a meal for any of a number of nocturnal meat eaters. Watch for their snow holes in forest openings.

Pheasants cling close to their food source and cover in late fall, especially if the ground is blanketed with snow.

Locate these concentrations of pheasant before expending a lot of your energy. Once you have located pheasant in snow, you can keep tabs on them all day. A good place to start looking is in a willow or cattail swamp.

Whitetails are far less inclined to cross openings after snow is on the ground. Look for them in thick cover, particularly cedar swamps.

Red fox will often be up and hunting in midday during a snowfall.

Jackrabbits are easier to hunt in really deep snow. They are not so scattered. They seek shelter from the winter winds along fence lines and under old farm machinery. Willow swamps are favorite hangouts for both food and shelter.

Predators are very susceptible to varmint calls during periods of deep snow. However, the hunter must take special pains to conceal himself.

In snow, shelter is more important to game birds and animals as well as predators. Foxes will always select a spot to bed down where they are sheltered from the wind, and other animals and birds are inclined to do the same. If they can combine this shelter from the wind with winter sunshine, so much the better.

About the only critter who doesn't seem to give a hoot about the snow, cold, wind, and rain is the snowshoe hare; in fact, as the snow grows deeper, he is able to reach higher for food of bark and twig ends.

My friend, Dennis Seline, who spends a lot of time in the winter trailing bobcat and coyote with hounds, walked out of the woods recently with the end of his shotgun barrel blown away. The culprit was snow in the barrel. Under the right conditions, snow will turn to ice in a gun barrel in minutes. Check your shotgun or rifle barrel frequently. If it contains snow, stop immediately and rectify the condition. Start by unloading the weapon. Sometimes all it takes to clear the barrel is to rap it against a tree trunk with the end of the barrel pointed down. If that doesn't do it, then it will be necessary to poke a slim sapling through the barrel, in the case of a shotgun, or a weed stalk with a rifle. I have cleaned out many a .22 rimfire rifle barrel with a weed stalk. Just be certain that no portion of the makeshift cleaning rod remains in the barrel. A better solution is to carry a breakdown cleaning rod, along with general emergency gear, in a day pack.

Severe cold can cause a rifle or shotgun to malfunction. Automatic rifles are particularly susceptible to jamming in cold weather. The culprit is lubricant grown stiff. Even the firing pin in a bolt-action rifle can be slowed so that it will not strike the primer hard enough to fire. There are two solutions. Both start with removing every trace of oil. The first solution is to simply leave the rifle or shotgun oil-free during the hunt. You can, of course, have the outer, unmoving parts, protected by oil or grease. The second solution is to use one of the lubricants designed expressly for cold temperatures. These are available at hardware and sporting-goods stores.

In cold weather, cameras are touchy, too. When possible, load a new roll of film in your camera indoors, before heading out to take photos of your winter adventures. Film gets very brittle in severe cold. Advance the film slowly to prevent breakage and scratching of the film. Battery contacts should be clean. Clean with a pencil eraser. The battery should be up to full strength. Carry a spare. If the camera shutter jams, get the camera into a warm place. Once thawed, the shutter can usually be released by jarring the camera lightly. Avoid breathing on the viewfinder or lens as these will easily fog up. Keep the camera dry. When carrying my camera in a day pack or belt pouch, I first seal it in a ziplock plastic bag.

Because hunting in snow requires extra energy and special precautions against getting lost, it pays to carry a light day pack, army cartridge belt with pockets, or a belt pouch with energy food and emergency gear. But keep it light. Priority items include food (chocolate bars, food sticks), waterproof match box, matches, compass, and knife. Extras include disinfectant, candle, salt, gun-cleaning rod (you can use a small lead sinker with string attached to pull a rag through the barrel), signal mirror, hatchet, metal cup, and bouillon. A canteen of water can be a lifesaver. Eating snow is unsatisfactory. A day

Specialized clothing is sometimes called for. Here a young Wisconsin hunter heads for an area where he plans to call foxes. (Photo courtesy Norman Johnson)

pack rides easier on a light packframe. The packframe must not ride above the shoulders, as it will snag on overhead limbs. A belt pouch is less of a nuisance; it does not have the carrying capacity of a day pack but has the advantage of lightness.

I have never experienced snow blindness. Sunglasses will help to prevent eye ache caused by snow glare. A visored cap is also helpful. Arctic travelers should darken the skin just below their eyes with charred embers from a fire; it will reduce glare.

Whether you reach your hunting site in a sports car or 4-wheel-drive vehicle, keep it in tune. Cold weather is hard on vehicles. Carry plenty of extras, including battery jumper cables, shovel, sand, tire chains, extra heater hose and antifreeze, and anything else that will help to get your vehicle started and out of a difficult situation. A heavy-duty truck bumper jack will get you out of many a tough spot.

Whether on a hunting trip or business, or just taking a Sunday drive, it is a good idea to carry emergency gear in your car during the winter months. For example, a snowmobile suit and one or two down sleeping bags kept in the car will come in very handy should you and your family be stranded in a blizzard. Spending a night in a car in sub-zero weather is no picnic. Sticking with your vehicle is normally the safest thing to do, unless a farm or other house is in sight. A couple of fat candles will help to heat the interior of a car. There is plenty of room to keep nonperishable food and emergency gear for injuries.

SIX

Hunting on Snowshoes

Dick Beck and I were hunting for foxes in farming country west of Minneapolis. Snow in the fields lay deep, but there was a crust on the surface and snowshoeing was easy. Typically, there was no snow crust in the woodlots and marshes. It was late in the day, and cutting through a woodlot would be a shortcut to Dick's pickup camper. Snowshoeing was not as pleasant in the soft snow. Dick was ahead of me and suddenly he disappeared.

I stayed on his trail. A dark hole appeared in the snow. Then I saw Dick's rifle barrel waving above the hole. He'd taken a spill and the snow depth was so great he was lost to view. It took our combined efforts to get him on his feet.

Dick Beck remembers the experience vividly, and ever since has carried a ski pole while snowshoeing. A ski pole is an advantage when maneuvering on snowshoes in brush. It serves as a prop when traversing a barbed wire fence and when walking up a steep slope. It can also serve as a rifle rest. It comes in handy, too, if you have taken a fall and are trying to get back on your feet.

Snowshoes were invented by the American Indian. They varied in design depending on where the individual tribe lived. The features of any particular tribe's snowshoe were dictated by tradition, available materials, and by the prevailing snow conditions.

Any normally healthy person can get the hang of snowshoeing in minutes. Knowing how to walk is basic to snowshoeing. The finer points of technique can be learned while doing. The snowshoe is designed to hold a person's foot firmly, preventing sideways motion, while allowing the foot to pivot forward freely. The toe dips into an opening in the shoe. The snowshoe is generally made of varnished strips of cowhide stretched over a curved wooden frame. Some snowshoes are now made with nylon reinforced neoprene, which does not stretch and will not collect ice.

The larger the area of the snowshoe, the more weight it will support without sinking too much into the snow. For a fairly heavy adult this would, in my opinion, eliminate the standard bear-paw snowshoe. However, the normally uncurved toe of the bear-paw shoe can be an advantage when climbing a steep slope. The straight toe can be kicked into the slope, giving the climber a flat surface to stand on. There are modified bear paws that feature a slight up-curve to the toe and a short tail. By dragging in the snow, the tail of a snowshoe provides stability. The greater curve of the toe, the less chance there is of the toe catching in the snow during normal walking. The standard bear-paw snowshoe is about 13×33 inches. It is ideal for maneuvering in thick growth. The bear-paw style has long been popular in the East, especially New England.

For 20 years my winter hunting was devoted almost exclusively to jackrabbits and foxes in the open, gently rolling farm country of southern and western Minnesota. The country is similar to that found throughout much of the Midwest and Plains states. I wore the Alaskan (pickeral) style snowshoe, 10×56 inches. Because of their narrow width, I could walk naturally. The long tail of the snowshoe, which remains in contact with the snow, provides stability. They were, and still are, perfectly suited for this kind of hunting and terrain. Often the snow in the fields would develop a crust. Under these conditions I could travel faster on snowshoes than I could on foot on bare ground.

When I moved to the northern forested part of Minnesota, I expected I would have to buy the bear paw or similar snowshoe designed for use in woods. I was surprised to find the Alaskan model to be just as popular in the northern forests as they were in the open farm country. The Michigan and cross-country styles, which are very similar, were also used. The long, narrow snowshoe is certainly not easy to navigate in brush, but I soon found myself getting used to this, and I simply did not try to make sharp corners. The very narrowness of the snowshoes I found to be an advantage in slipping through closely spaced aspen and alder. I wear them for hunting snowshoe hares and bobcats.

I have a difficult time with my pickeral snowshoes on steep inclines. They are also awkward to wear when doing odd jobs around the yard or camp. Here, I think, the bear paw would be ideal. Because of their length, pickeral snowshoes are awkward to carry on one's back.

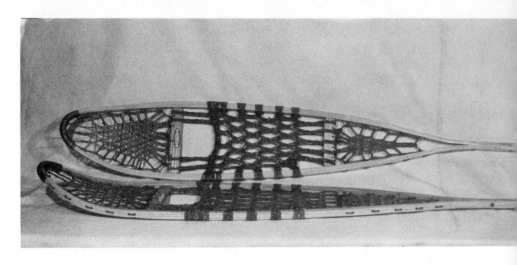

The Alaskan (pickeral) snowshoe, 10x56 inches. The author's favorite. (Photo courtesy L. L. Bean, Inc.)

But for most hunting in snow they do the job.

The Maine snowshoe is probably the best compromise between the long, narrow shoe and the short, wide shoe. The dimensions of the Maine shoe run 11×42, 12×42, and 13×48 inches. Choice depends on your weight.

The following descriptions were excerpted from a mail-order catalog and will give the reader an idea of what is available in sporting-goods stores and from mail-order houses:

Modified Bear-Paw Snowshoe: Use nylon neoprene lacings for longer life and extra strength. They have a strong white ash frame shaped to combine the bear-paw's compactness with a short tail to prevent twist.

Two sizes:

12×34 inches (for persons weighing 125 to 165 pounds)
14×36 inches (for persons weighing 165 to 215 pounds)

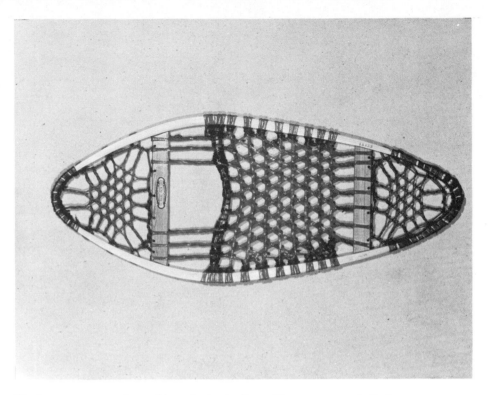

The bear-paw snowshoe. A favorite in the East. (Photo courtesy L. L. Bean, Inc)

The Maine Snowshoe: The frames are of specially selected second-growth white ash butts seasoned so they will not warp. The filling is the very best cowhide cured by a secret process that positively prevents sagging. The toe is reinforced with rawhide. The workmanship gives the shoe perfect balance.

Three sizes:

12×42 inches (for persons weighing 125 to 165 pounds)
13×48 inches (for persons weighing 165 to 225 pounds)
11×40 inches (for children)

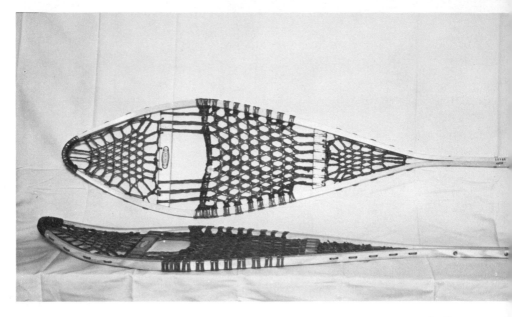

The Maine snowshoe. A good compromise. (Photo courtesy L. L. Bean, Inc)

Bear-Paw Snowshoe: It is made from fine grain ash and has a slightly turned-up toe. The filling will not sag. They are very popular with guides, lumber cruisers, and trappers who are obliged to travel in thick growth.

Size: 13×35 inches

Pickeral Snowshoe: This narrow shoe is made of the same high-grade material used in the Maine Snowshoe. It had its origin with the Indians of the Far North, who needed a light, easy-running shoe to track down game on light, drifting snow. The narrow tread and high upturn reduces interference and tripping. It does not load, and its bearing value is equal to other types of shoes half again as wide.

Size: 10×56 inches

Trail Model Snowshoe: This is a sturdy, long-tailed snowshoe designed to support heavy and tall men. Its medium width, high, turned-up toe performs perfectly in open and uphill travel, yet is not cumbersome in moderate growth.

Size: 12×60 inches

Cross-Country Snowshoe: It has long been popular with bobcat and rabbit hunters, but is now in wide use because its compact size is particularly comfortable for recreational snowshoeing.

Size: 10×46 inches

My present snowshoe harness is made of leather and is homemade. It is designed after a commercial model worn earlier. When I replace my harness I will buy a commercial model that combines leather with neoprene. Nylon-reinforced neoprene will not slip or stretch, as leather does. I lean toward buying a harness that features a toe "pocket" that prevents the toe from slipping forward on steep descents and eliminates the possibility of wobbly or loose snowshoes.

I carry a spare harness. This is simply a six-foot clothesline rope. I tie something akin to a squaw hitch, laying the center of the rope across the back of my ankle, bringing the ends forward and around the stout framing by my toe. The rope is then crisscrossed over my toe and the ends brought back behind the ankle and tied. This will last for two or three days of tough walking.

Another advantage of snowshoes over skis is that most any kind of boot can be worn. The only consideration is that they be reasonably waterproof and warm. With snowshoes I have worn overshoes, rubber-bottomed pacs, and the Air Force "bunny boot." I rather like the bunny boot because of its stiffness; there is no pressure on my feet from the bindings.

When snowshoeing, try a long, gliding gait. Relax

The author on snowshoes carries out a fox in the last fading light of day.

and take your time. Don't try to lift your snowshoes high above the snow—a sliding motion will do it. Your heel should rise with the forward stride, and your toe pivot downward through the toe pocket of the snowshoe. Snowshoeing uses the muscles in the anterior portion of your leg. If you aren't used to snowshoeing, you will get pretty tired the first few times. Be comforted by the knowledge that you would be more tired without them.

SEVEN

Cold-Weather Clothing

When I poked my nose out of the old line shack that morning, there was no real way to gauge how cold it was without a thermometer. One of the loggers, near where we were hunting bobcat, said it had dropped to 30 degrees below zero the night before. I retrieved my nose from the cold and began piling on every article of clothing I could find and then topped it all with an expedition parka of northern goosedown. I looked like a sentry on duty in the Arctic; in fact, I was ideally dressed for sentry duty, ice fishing, or all-day posting for deer.

Following a trailing hound in pursuit of bobcat you are aware that it is active hunting. Dennis Seline, whose dog Jerry would be doing the trailing, was fully aware of the activity that lay ahead. After donning the usual long underwear, wool pants, and a couple of layers of wool shirts, he was almost ready to go. His only conciliation to the cold was a goosedown vest under the outer wool shirt.

It was cool that day, but my heat loss through perspiration was so great, and my clothing so damp, that had I been lost, I would have had a miserable night in the woods. Hunting in snow is often active hunting. The most common mistake is to wear too many clothes.

Wool does a good job of handling moisture, but no kind of clothing can disperse a lot of perspiration. You can handle almost any cold-weather situation, including a night in the cold winter woods, if your clothing is dry and reasonably adequate. Wet clothing is disastrous. I doubt I have ever been more dehydrated on the hottest summer day than I was that winter day. A canteen of water would have done a lot to alleviate the situation. The principal danger of dehydration is that in an emergency situation it aggravates the syndromes of shock and hypothermia (exposure). You can avoid heavy perspiring by wearing clothing in layers and peeling off each layer *before*, not after, you start to perspire. This extra clothing can be stuffed into a daypack, belt pouch, or tied with twine and slung over your shoulder. You will want to put it back on during prolonged rest stops.

The body is better able to deal with serious situations during the day if kept adequately supplied with food and water. Heat is produced from food, so carry a generous supply of chocolate bars or trail snacks on cold-weather hunting trips, and keep nibbling all day. If you are going to camp out overnight, food in your stomach will help keep you warm during the night. Fatty foods are particularly good heat producers. Chances are you will never have to deal with a serious situation in cold weather. Most hunters today do not stray far from the road. It is a comfort, though, to be informed and prepared.

Insulation

We have discussed preventing heat loss through per-spiration, but most hunters are concerned with heat loss that results from inadequate clothing. To prevent heat from escaping from the body it is necessary to trap air and hold it. This trapped air is the real insulation. The more layers of this trapped air, the warmer you will be. The weight of the layer is of no benefit. Two fuzzy sweaters of medium weight are better than a heavy one weighing the same amount, because they provide two layers of trapped air. I like to buy old, out-of-style sweaters at garage sales. If they hang well below my waist and are several sizes too large, so much the better. Loose-fitting clothing traps more air.

Northern goosedown is the best insulator. It is best used for severe cold, when the layer system would require so many layers as to be too heavy. The hard, synthetic outer material of a goosedown parka is great for cutting winter winds in open terrain. Goosedown is ideal for situations in which the hunter must stand for long periods. A lot of thick clothing is needed for pro-longed standing in severe cold. Even then you may have to move occasionally.

For most late season and winter hunting situations, the layer system can be used, especially layers of wool. Wool is still the winter hunter's best friend. Goosedown loses its insulating qualities if it gets wet. Wool, even if you have broken through lake ice, still offers some insulation. It is ideal for when rain changes to snow. Also, the synthetic coverings on goosedown coats are noisy in brush. Wool is silent.

Cold Weather and the Deer Hunter

For many years I wore a red wool coat for deer hunting. It was very heavy and soured me on wool. If I had known then what I know now, I'd have bought a good wool shirt instead. I'd have bought it large enough to have worn other wool shirts or sweaters beneath it. I'd have taken pains to find light, fuzzy sweaters and shirts to wear under the wool shirt, because it is thickness, not weight, that counts. November and December are the major deer-hunting months in most states. Weather conditions will fluctuate from one extreme to the other at this time. The deer hunter must be prepared for anything.

Don't make the mistake that because last year's deer hunting was warm and pleasant, this year will be the same. In my own state, conditions during the month-long period when deer-hunting dates could be chosen, varied from 70 degrees above zero and sunny skies, to minus 15 degrees and snow on the ground. In between, it fluctuated between drizzling rain, wet snow that stuck to every twig and bush, and dry snow that drifted slowly down in sub-zero temperatures.

The following is an outfit I like for basic deer hunting. It keeps me fairly comfortable in a wide range of temperatures and stays relatively dry in drizzling rain or wet snow. It serves for up to two hours of trail watching, or all day if still-hunting. (I define still-hunting as moving slowly through the woods with frequent long pauses.) I start with shorts and T-shirt. Next I put on long underwear top and bottom. This is of double construction. It has an inner layer of comfortable cotton,

This hunter is not only dressed warmly, he wears the new 3M air warming mask. During wear tests the mask raises the temperature of inhaled air to an average 60 degrees above zero with 95 percent humidity from a 20 degree below zero, 10 percent humidity environment. (Photo courtesy 3M Company)

For really cold weather, waterproof boots with thick felt liners are good. It is necessary that felt liners and felt inner soles be dried nightly. (Photo courtesy L. L. Bean, Inc)

while the outer layer is 40 percent worsted wool, 50 percent cotton and 10 percent nylon. Next come socks, pants, and shirt. These items are 85 percent wool and 15 percent nylon. I like either an all-rubber boot, or a light leather boot with rubber bottoms. Of the two, I prefer the leather boot with rubber bottom and felt inner sole for cool, late-season hunting. I find a standard cap with visor and ear flaps that fit to be adequate for most deer-hunting conditions.

The remainder of my outfit, worn over the long underwear top and wool shirt, will vary with the conditions. Another wool shirt may be all that is required. If it is pretty nippy, I'll wear a goosedown vest between the two wool shirts. A turtleneck dickey prevents heat loss around my open shirt top. I wear leather chopper mitts with wool liners. If the weather is mild, I leave my shooting hand bare. If the day grows warm, I store chopper mitts in a belt pouch, where I carry a light, waterproof shell parka to slip on if rain or wet snow gets heavy.

If planning an all-day vigil of trail watching for deer, I dress more warmly. For this I like plenty of goosedown padding. Snowmobile suits are good, all-day wear. So is a roomy rubber-bottomed pack boot with thick felt liners. You have to be prepared for anything when deer hunting.

I wear a goosedown parka on winter fox and jackrabbit hunts that take me out into cold, windswept terrain. The hood is a lifesaver under conditions of very severe wind. It really traps body heat. The body does not shut down the blood supply to the head when temperatures drop, as it does to other extremities. One can easily pump over half of one's body heat into the cold winter air through an uncovered head. A good cold-weather hat is the fur-lined hat with ear muffs that can be tied on top of the hat or lowered over the ears. A wool face mask like those worn by skiers can feel very good in extreme wind and cold. A turtleneck dickey or sweater will help retain body heat around an open neck and coat top.

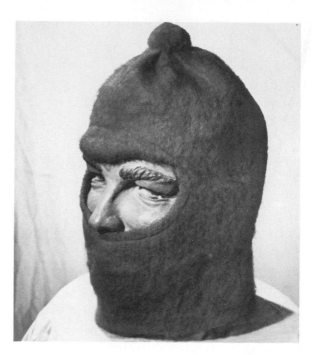

Top The Balaclava helmet is great for severe conditions of wind and cold. (Photo courtesy L. L. Bean, Inc)

Above A cap like this will provide warmth and protection in the severest cold. (Photo courtesy L. L. Bean, Inc)

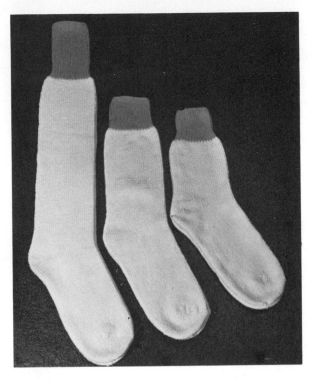

Wool socks are good but they need synthetic material added for strength and elasticity. Wool content should be 80 to 85 percent. (Photo courtesy L. L. Bean, Inc)

Here is a closer look at individual articles of clothing:

Socks: Avoid socks with a high cotton content. Cotton soaks up perspiration and holds it, becoming cool and clammy. Get wool socks with some nylon for strength. Wear a fresh pair each day. If this is not possible, take care to dry the used pair overnight.

Underwear: Cotton long underwear will absorb perspiration too, but it certainly is more comfortable than wool. An excellent cold-weather combination is the true net underwear, originated by Nordic fishermen using fishnets, under a pair of 85 percent wool and 15 percent

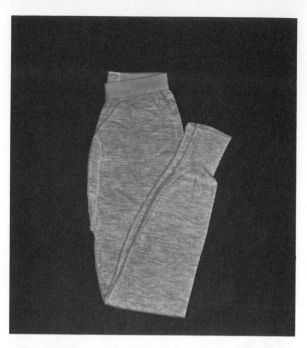

This long underwear features a layer of cotton on the inside with a percentage of wool in an outer layer. It's not as insulating as 100 percent wool, but a lot more comfortable. (Photo courtesy L. L. Bean, Inc)

nylon underwear. This combination forms cells of insulated air. It also provides a layer of air next to the body in which perspiration can vaporize. The fishnet–wool combination would be a good idea for the hunter planning a prolonged bivouac. I'm not a stickler on long underwear. The double-layer kind with cotton on the inside and some wool in the outer layer is good enough for me.

Pants: Wool is best. If the pants will be taking a lot of abuse, a hard-finished wool or Orlon with synthetic added will prolong wear. Blue jeans are absolutely worthless for wet and snow.

Shirts and sweaters: Wool or Orlon. Tightly woven

Top A turtleneck dickey gives surprising warmth, yet can easily be removed as the day warms. (Photo courtesy L. L. Bean, Inc)

Above Wool shirts and pants are the winter hunter's best friend. (Photo courtesy L. L. Bean, Inc)

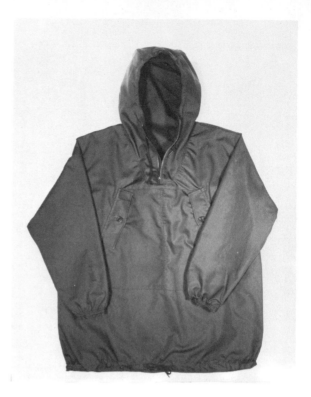

A parka like this can provide shelter from wind, rain, and cold, yet be light in weight. (Photo courtesy L. L. Bean, Inc)

shirts and sweaters will wear better, but fuzzy, loosely knit garments provide the best insulation. Loose, baggy-fitting clothing is better than tailored.

Shell clothing: Wind, rain, or snow (when excessive) call for a wind and rainproof outer shell, preferably a roomy parka with hood. Shell clothing can be very light weight. Wind-tight parkas that will shed some water are best made from cotton or nylon−cotton combinations.

Down clothing: It's expensive. Unless you plan to hunt in severe wind and cold, a down vest may be all you will ever need. Down becomes useless when wet, but this is

The down parka, the ultimate for severe cold or prolonged posting for deer or predators. (Photo courtesy L. L. Bean, Inc)

rarely a problem in very cold weather. Down clothing becomes necessary when the temperature drops so low that the amount of normal layer insulation needed would be unmanageably heavy, constricting, and bulky.

EIGHT

Winter Camping

Winter camping can be an enjoyable experience, but it takes more knowledge and somewhat better equipment to keep your camping trip from becoming a long-remembered disaster.

That word disaster is not uncommon when it comes to hunters describing their camping efforts. It is not so difficult when a pickup camper or trailer is employed. It is when you get into tent camping that you hear the real tales of woe: malfunctioning oil and gas stoves, inadequate heaters, smoke-filled tents, and nights spent in bitter discomfort. Yet I prefer camping in fall or winter to any other season.

For many years I stayed away from using a tent for deer hunting and other cold-weather activities. Then one day I was admiring pictures of old-time deer-hunting camps in Michigan's Upper Peninsula and Maine's Allagash country. I noticed how often big tents with woodburning stoves were used. I knew that similar camps are used today by many big-game outfitters in the western United States and Canada for deer and elk hunting. These outfitters charge a healthy sum for their services, and I could not imagine their providing hunters with an uncomfortable camp. I contacted my friend Norman Strung, an outdoor writer and guide based near Bozeman, Montana, and asked if a tent-stove arrangement was practical. He was encouraging and suggested that if my hunting camp was going to be semi-permanent that I go to an even larger tent size than the 10×13 model I planned to use. Norm has permanent tent frameworks built for his mountain hunting camps. He advised white canvas if possible for a lighter, brighter interior. I wanted mobility and stuck with my 10×13 model—a light, summer tent of A-wall design.

I bought a lightweight sheet-metal stove called an Airtight, commonly found in hardware stores. The manufacturer is Jackes-Evans Manufacturing Company, 11737 Administration Road, St. Louis, Missouri 63141. Airtight stoves come in three sizes. I got the middle size. The smallest size would have been sufficient to heat the tent, but I wanted one that could handle limbs up to 20 inches. I did not want to have to depend on pre-cut wood. My stove is approximately 24 inches high with the detachable legs in place. It is 21 inches long by 15 inches wide and weighs only eight pounds. The Airtight stove, while lightweight, is a bulky item. The price was right, however. In 1972 it cost only $11. Fold-up stoves are available. Sims Stoves, Department C, Lovell, Wyoming 82431, offers models from (at the time of this writing) $33.60–$60 that fold up to only 3½-inch thickness and fit into a canvas case.

I get almost immediate heat from my stove. The thin sheet metal gives radiant heat and can turn the icy interior of the tent warm and comfortable in minutes.

The heat can be controlled, but if things get too warm (the only problem) I simply throw open the tent door or open a window. We commonly sit around in T-shirts and shorts in temperatures that are close to 80 degrees above zero inside and 20 degrees below zero outside. Allow the fire to go out, however, and the tent's interior temperature is quickly the same as that outdoors. During cold weather, I will periodically throw a log in the fire during the night. It is surprising, though, how often one can let the fire go out and sleep comfortably. I keep kindling within reach and can get a fire started without leaving my sleeping bag. With frequent use of my stove, I have become increasingly adept at maintaining a uniform temperature.

Obviously this is not the kind of camping one does on foot. I have camped some distance from backcountry roads in winter by hauling my gear in by toboggan. This is hard, time-consuming work, and I only do it if I plan to stay for five days or more. A couple of times I left my camp on public land for weeks, using it only off and on during that time. Leaving your camp unattended is risky, but there are many woodland spots that never see a human track in winter. Snowmobilers pretty well stick to well-defined trails.

In addition to my 50-pound tent, and the bulk of stove and stove pipes, I use cots, four-inch foam pads on the cots, two small tables and camp stove, lantern, and some dry wood from home. I also made a base for the wood stove. This is necessary to prevent burning a hole through the bottom of the tent. I nailed a 30×37-inch fireboard to ¾-inch plywood. I screwed "L"-shaped screws into this board to hold the stove legs secure.

The key to comfort is the woodburning stove, and the key to feeling comfortable with such an arrangement—

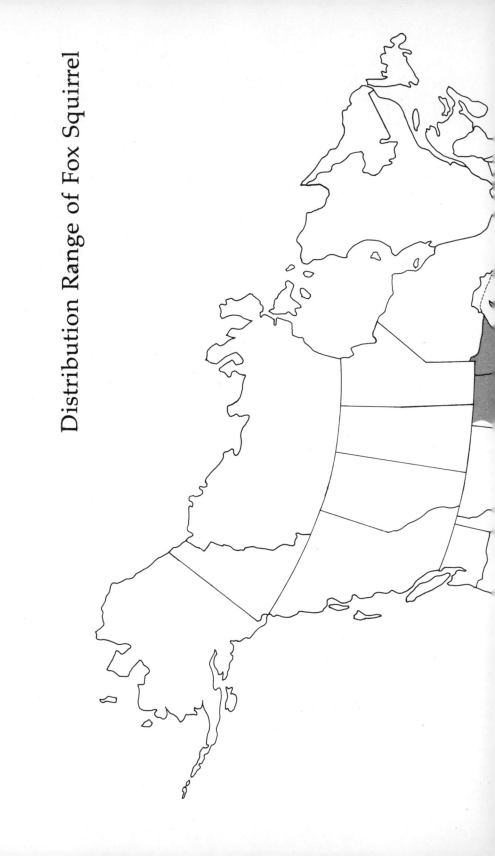

Distribution Range of Fox Squirrel

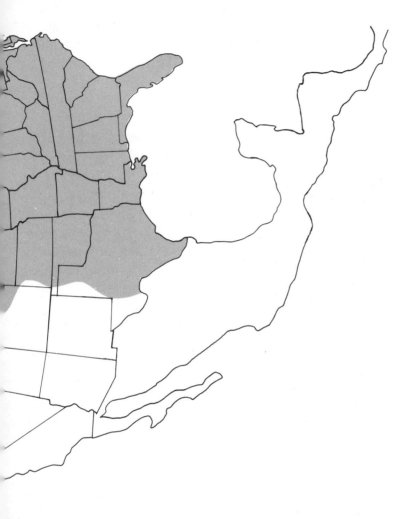

an arrangement that could easily burn your tent to the ground—is in setting it up properly. I have the stovepipe coming out the back of the tent about 1½ feet from the peak. In cutting the opening for the stovepipe, I first set the stove in place on the fireboard almost in the center of the tent. I then place the pipe so that after first rising straight up from the stove, it then curves toward the back wall of the tent. Two elbow pipes are used because I needed extra height. Where the pipe touches the canvas, I cut a hole approximately two inches wider than circumference of the pipe. Around this hole, and on the outside of the tent, I have a flashing of the correct size for the stovepipe used. Between the flashing and the canvas are two sheets of asbestos cut to the same shape as the flashing. On the inside of the tent I use two sheets of asbestos under sheet metal cut to the shape of the flashing. Short screws are inserted through holes punched through the outside sheet metal and asbestos clear through the tent canvas and the asbestos and sheet metal on the inside, and snugged tight with washers and nuts. On summer campouts, when the stove is not in use, I stuff a rag in the stovepipe opening to keep out insects and moisture.

When using the woodburning stove I insert the end of the inside stovepipe into the stovepipe hole. It is a snug fit. Outside the tent, I add an elbow pipe to the flashing. On this I set a straight stovepipe. The top of this pipe is 12 inches above the tent. This outside pipe is clamped to the ridge-brace pole with hose clamps available at hardware and auto-parts stores. It is necessary to use two of these clamps together in order to go around your five- or six-inch stovepipe and tent pole. Clamping or tying the outside stovepipe to the ridge-brace pole is very important. This holds the stovepipe rigidly in place.

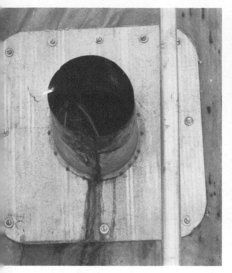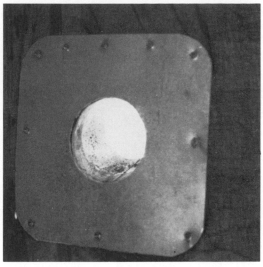

ABOVE LEFT Flashing in place on outside of tent wall.
ABOVE RIGHT Stovepipe hole as seen from inside of tent.

Two cots provide a nice seating and sleeping arrangement for two. Mine are the old-style army cot. We have had four people in our tent during deer hunts. Two of the hunters slept on foam pads on the floor. During the day their sleeping gear was stored under the cots. In the long winter evenings, four people can sit or lounge on the cots. There is room to get up and move around.

Avoid pitching your tent in open spots that can become windswept during a storm. The greatest hazard is in your tent collapsing while there is a fire in the stove. The stovepipe can pull loose in a buffeting wind.

Always bring some dry wood from home. Wet weather may make it difficult to cut dry wood. Dry wood is particularly useful for getting a fire going on a cold morning. I like to camp near logging sites. There

ABOVE LEFT Outside stovepipe in place. Note that it is tied to tent pole. Two hose clamps used together work better. Hose clamps should go completely around pipe and tent pole.

ABOVE RIGHT Woodburning stove in place.

are always scrap tree tips and limbs available for burning.

Often overlooked, but absolutely essential in cold-weather camping, is making provisions for drying garments wet or dampened by snow or perspiration during the day's hunting exertions. This is a difficult problem if your tent has outside poles, as most do. One solution is an extra ridge pole on the inside of the tent, just for

My tent-stove camp ready for a winter hunt.

drying clothes. The colder the temperature the more important that hunting clothes be thoroughly dried each night. Socks and boot liners are important items to keep dry. The liners of buckskin chopper mitts should be removed and dried nightly. They may feel dry, but simple perspiration can cause cold hands the next day.

With a four-inch foam pad on my cot, I sleep in comfort. This pad is not just a luxury item, because air circulating under the cot makes a cold bed. My old goosedown sleeping bag is so old and matted that I find greater comfort by combining two summer sleeping bags. The filling in these bags is a much cheaper, less insulating material but the two bags combined work out well.

I have no doubt that when I buy a new bag I will get a quality down bag. A down bag with nylon shell is a good cold-weather investment. Down provides more insulation per unit weight than any other material. Down-insulated bags breathe well. Down can be compressed again and again, returning each time to essentially the same volume. But remember, even the best sleeping bag will not keep you warm without something underneath it. There are three kinds of ground insulation: the open cell foam pad with a cover, which is the most expensive and comfortable; the standard air mattress, which is too cold for most winter use; and closed cell foam, which is warm and has a low price tag.

"If your feet are cold, put on your hat." That sounds ridiculous but it is based on solid fact. High-blood circulation is maintained in the surface skin of the head, even when the body is cold. This can result in tremendous losses of heat. Knowledgeable winter campers wear a stocking cap when they sleep. Another good idea is to slip on clean wool socks and long underwear before retiring.

Pickup campers and trailers have one big advantage over tent camping: there is no hassle getting things set up. This is a real break when you plan to camp for only one or two nights. They are easy to heat, usually with bottled gas, and many are equipped with stove, sink, and refrigerator. They have the disadvantage of being limited to substantial roads; also, gas mileage is poor.

A pickup camper lacks the luxuries, but in a pickup with just a topper, you can tackle backroads and still have a fairly comfortable sleeping arrangement. Cooking, of course, is limited to a gas or propane stove on the back tailgate.

You can add to the comfort and economy of winter

A pickup camper packs a lot of comfort into winter camping and hunting trips.

camping with tent, pickup camper, tent camper, or travel trailer with these winter camping tips:

Dry wood, brought from home, will quickly ignite a winter campfire or kindle the morning fire in a wood-burning stove. Almost every garage and basement contain wood scraps. Large pieces can be baled, small scraps bagged. Mesh potato or onion sacks are good for bagging small scraps of wood.

Economize on fuel used to operate heaters in pickup camper and travel trailer with an electric heater. Electrical outlets are sometimes available at no charge. Leave your refrigerator turned off. Two one-gallon plastic containers of ice stored in the fridge will keep food and beverages cool on a weekend trip. As the water melts it can be used for coffee or washing dishes.

You can still barbecue outside in winter. Charcoal is quickly ignited when the coals are stored in paper egg cartons. Each carton containing a dozen briquettes should be tied with twine. When soaked with fuel, these burn freely, and quickly start the makings of a winter barbecue.

Because it is imperative to provide ventilation with gas and other heaters in pickup campers and trailers, some cool air will be concentrated along the floor in even the warmest trailer. Keep socks and other clothing to be worn the next day up high to avoid discomfort.

Insulated containers used to keep items cold in summer can be utilized to keep potatoes and other vegetables from freezing in winter.

NINE

Predator Calling

Calling is not as hard to master as many would have you think. The predator call imitates cottontails and hares, both of which are important winter food items for coyotes and bobcats. The difficult part is getting positioned properly, where your quarry won't see or hear you. Because of the wide open spaces in most parts of the West, the caller can generally find a good vantage point where he can see in all directions. Be especially careful to watch downwind, since coyotes will invariably approach from that direction. Be prepared to shoot if the predator approaches from downwind, because he might catch your scent and spook anytime.

Coyotes are exceedingly wary creatures, but it's amazing how they'll gallop straight to a caller who is well hidden. Good spots for calling are in areas where there are plenty of brushy draws that support plenty of rabbits, and sites where deer are concentrated in their winter range. Coyotes make no bones about hanging close to deer, and they take a great toll each winter.

Winston Burnham calling predators. (Photo courtesy Russell Tinsley)

Predator callers often have success around those areas. Bobcats are not as common as coyotes and are called infrequently. Unlike coyotes that may appear in packs of a half dozen or more, bobcats come in singly. They are sneaky and use every available piece of cover as they approach. They take longer to come in than coyotes. Figure about twenty minutes in a good bobcat area. Coyotes will come in within ten minutes. If they aren't in by then, there are none within earshot of the call, or they are wise. Bobcat calling can be effective in high altitudes, where there are numerous snowshoe hares. Hares are often the exclusive winter diet of bobcats. Tracks in the snow will indicate the presence of cats.

Winter is the hungry time of year for predators, and the best time of all for predator calling. Coyotes seem to be less wary during the winter months. Maybe the cold weather sharpens their appetites and makes them eager for an easy meal. Also, in mid-winter their pelts are in prime condition. Predators skin out 200 percent easier when they're still hot.

In recent years the pelt value of long-furred animals such as fox, coyote, bobcat, and raccoon has soared. Dennis Seline shipped ten bobcat pelts to a fur auction in 1974 and averaged $65 a pelt. In 1975–76, bobcats were selling for $80 to $100 and higher in Canada. Coyotes and fox have brought $15 to $65 in recent years.

Permissible winter hunting methods vary greatly between the states. Some states permit night hunting with a light in the winter only. January and February are the top months for hunting fox in certain Mountain States in the West. Where shooting after dark is legal, the best calling hours are from dusk to midnight. A red-lens light is superior to conventional white. Tests have proved that animals are oblivious to the red beam; put another way, they cannot see the light, since red photographed with black-and-white film comes out black. With a red light you can put the beam directly on an

In a Michigan field, Frank Martin calls foxes by squeaking through the fingers of his hand. Frank is now based in Montana and calling in coyotes with the same method. (Photo courtesy Frank Martin)

incoming animal without spooking it. For actual shooting, however, it is best to switch to a more brilliant white light.

After a fresh snowfall, tracks give graphic evidence of the presence of foxes, bobcats, or coyotes, and a hunter doesn't have to waste valuable calling time in areas that lack prospective targets. Also, the animals are much easier to spot against a white background.

A good, flat-shooting handgun like this Ruger .44 Magnum plus a pair of good calls equal one prime coyote pelt. (Photo courtesy Clair Rees)

The dying-rabbit call is the only winter standby, because rabbits provide a primary food source in the wintertime. Also good is a bird-in-distress cry, since some birds like the meadowlark roost on the ground and are actively sought by hungry predators. The bird-distress call is especially effective on raccoons.

Moon phase has a definite influence on calling, even during the wintertime. For instance, if the moon comes up late and is still visible in the sky after daybreak, morning calling usually will be more productive; but if the moon rises before dark, late-afternoon hunting normally pays off best.

Texas hunter Russell Tinsley uses predator call from natural blind. (Photo courtesy Russell Tinsley)

TEN

Trapping

Setting out a few traps does not take much time but it can add profit, pleasure, and adventure to any hunting trip. Rarely does a season go by that I do not find the time to run a short trap line. If I have any complaint about trapping it is that it often threatens to cut into my hunting time.

One of trapping's greatest attractions is the opportunity it gives for seeing all kinds of game. I once became so involved examining mink tracks below an overhanging bank that upon rising I saw a red fox only ten feet away. I have often seen mink along stream banks, and I once found a cottontail that had accidentally hung itself in the fork of a bush. One evening a great horned owl tried to carry away my stocking cap—along with my scalp.

Great expectations are another of trapping's fascinations. Will that new set produce? It all depends, of course, on how well you read the sign, tracks, trails, and droppings. It depends, too, on using equipment free of

This Pennsylvania trapper is looking for signs of furbearers. (Photo courtesy J. E. Osman, Pennsylvania Game Commission)

foreign odors, and the careful placing and concealing of the trap. Nothing will get you closer to the earth and wildlife than trapping.

Traps

For muskrat, I like the No. 1 size Victor and the Blake & Lamb stop-loss trap. Also the No. 110 Victor Conibear and No. 1 Blake & Lamb sure-grip trap. The stop-loss trap prevents muskrats from twisting free. The muskrat, more than any other furbearer, is capable of escaping from the steel trap. The sure-grip and body-grip traps are designed to grip the animal about the neck or chest, killing it instantly.

For mink and raccoon, I like the high quality of the Victor coil-spring trap in No. 1½ size. It is easy to conceal yet has great holding power, and is also excellent for marten, skunk, and opossum.

For fox, the Victor and Blake & Lamb No. 2 coil-springs are usually rated tops. These traps work beautifully with the popular "dirt-hole" set that has been luring in foxes and coyotes for years.

For coyote, I like the Oneida and Blake & Lamb No. 3 underspring (jump trap) and double longspring.

For beaver, try the Oneida and Blake & Lamb No. 4 in either underspring or double longspring. An excellent choice, where it can be used, is the Victor Conibear No. 330 body-grip trap. This is a killer-type trap and must be handled with extreme caution because it could break an arm.

I like steel fur stretchers for muskrat, and homemade wood stretchers for other furbearers. You can get the idea of how wooden fur stretchers are shaped by examining commercial wire stretchers. Fur stretchers and steel traps are sold in hardware and sporting-goods stores and trappers' supply houses. It pays to visit your

Author's son, Dave Gilsvik, scouts a beaver lodge for its trapping possibilities.

The end result is a prime beaver. (Photo courtesy J. E. Osman, Pennsylvania Game Commission)

Author's brother Rich Gilsvik nails up a beaver pelt to dry. Beaver pelts are difficult for the beginner to handle.

local fur buyer. He will answer your questions about fur stretchers and may lend you some to use as models. It is to his advantage that you bring in well-handled pelts.

If you are not experienced in skinning, fleshing, and

128

drying pelts, do not let this deter you. If you are able to skin the furbearer, and do not have the necessary drying form (stretcher), roll the pelt into a ball, fur side out, seal in a plastic bag and store in your freezer. When you plan to sell the pelt, it can be thawed at room temperature and sold green (not dried). Fur buyers will even buy animals that have not been skinned; generally they deduct a small amount from the pelt value. Skinning, fleshing, and drying of pelts are skills you will want to acquire, however.

Dyeing and Waxing Traps

When trappers buy new and shiny traps, they bury them in mud. The object is to allow rust to develop and lightly corrode the metal. This is necessary in order to darken the traps later with bark or wood dye. Traps are boiled in a tub of water as the first step in the darkening process. Then some of the surface water is poured off to remove oil and rust that has risen to the surface. Then bark from native trees (except pine) can be added or a commercial trapper's wood dye used. The wood dye really does the job. Allow the solution to boil for several hours, then let the traps remain in this for several days to more permanently etch the dye into the metal. This is a job best done outdoors over an improvised fireplace.

The traps are now protected from further corrosion, are easier to conceal, and the smell of steel has been replaced by a woodsy, earthy odor. These traps are ready for action.

Some trappers like to wax their traps for further protection and faster action. Usually a commercial trapper's wax is used. This is melted in a narrow container deep enough to completely submerge a trap. Each trap is lowered into the smoking hot wax for at least a minute. Each trap must become as hot as the wax. Easier than waxing traps, which can be dangerous with smoking hot wax, is coating them with acrylic floor finish. It is cheap, safe to use, odorless, easy to apply, and dries to a hard plastic finish. Trappers simply dip their traps into a container filled with liquid acrylic or pour the liquid over the traps set in a container. The traps are then taken out and allowed to dry.

Preseason Scouting

If there is a big secret to successful trapping, aside from years of experience, it is knowing ahead of the season where you will set your traps. Generally, there are only a few weeks between the beginning of the trapping season—when furs are prime for harvesting—and freeze-up. When creeks freeze, mink trapping becomes very difficult. Raccoons will hibernate. Traps set for fox and coyote freeze to the ground. So the season's first few weeks offer the easiest trapping. With set locations, drowning wires, guide sticks, and other preparations and alterations done ahead of time, usually in late summer or early fall, you will save valuable time and make good catches right from the start. Pre season scouting—the examining of tracks, trails, droppings, and other signs of furbearing animals—is also fascinating.

Baits and Lures

If your trapping will be confined to water trapping for mink, muskrat, raccoon, or beaver, you can get by without bait or lure (scent). It is easy to find where these animals are entering or exiting the water, and to locate where they must walk or swim through narrow passageways. Simple blind sets can be made. A blind set is the placement of your trap where you believe the animal will step. As you gain in experience, you will want to experiment with bait and lure.

For the sly land animals—the fox, coyote, and wolf— bait and lure are used, although some catches can be made in trails or near where these animals are feeding on carrion. Commercial lures work best. The problem with most homemade lures is that they often scare away more animals than they attract.

Buy several brands of lure and see which works best on your trap line. The trapper of fox, coyote, and wolf will also want to buy urine of the animal to be trapped. This is a great suspicion remover. Where both red and gray fox are found, it is best to use red fox urine. Red fox are afraid of the gray fox and will be reluctant to approach a set where gray fox urine has been used. If fox and coyote overlap, stick with fox urine, because all foxes are afraid of the larger coyote and wolf. A lure that attracts one kind of canine will usually attract the others, including dogs.

Bait can be bought commercially, but most trappers make their own. For coyotes, wolves, and foxes, this bait should be slightly tainted. Bait can be flesh from a dead cow or horse, a road-killed deer, or an unprotected species of animal that you have shot. In some areas this could be such animals as woodchuck, jackrabbit, and prairie dog. Procure several animals a few weeks prior to the trapping season. Some trappers are careful to avoid handling the bait with their bare hands, using rubber gloves to banish human scent. Remove the entrails and, with a hatchet or meat cleaver, cut the carcasses into cubes about the size of marshmallows or walnuts. Do not skin the animals, and use all but the entrails, feet, and tail. Then put the cubes into clean fruit jars, screw the lids down tightly, and bury the jars under nine to ten inches of dirt in a cool, shaded spot. After a week to ten days, the bait will be slightly tainted and ready to use. Use one or two pieces to a set.

Muskrat

This is America's number-one furbearer. Trapped by the thousands each year, they are prolific and, in temperate zones, can breed at almost any time of year.

There are many possible set locations for muskrat along creeks, rivers, water-filled ditches, and marshes. Look for their droppings (similar to rabbit) on rocks and logs. Muskrats will climb onto these to enjoy a snack at leisure. The trapper can make an attractive set for muskrat by floating two logs in the water side by side. These should be six inches thick by three feet long and held together by crosspieces nailed across the ends. This floating raft is then anchored to the shoreline with wire. It is one set that will remain effective in fluctuating water levels. Bait will make this set even more attractive. Spear slices of apple, carrot, celery, or muskrat flesh (they are not entirely vegetarians) on short sticks and wedge them between the logs. Two or three traps can be set between the baited sticks. Traps should be anchored to the underside of the logs. This is a good drowning set for muskrat. Traps need not be covered, and even shiny, untreated traps will catch them. Still, it is a good idea to lay a light sprinkling of dry grass over the traps.

If you find where an old tree trunk slants out of the water, set a trap just below the water's surface, held lightly in place with nails. A few inches above the water nail bait of carrot, celery, apple, or muskrat flesh.

Muskrats like to swim in the safety of overhanging banks. Set a body-grip trap right up against the bank if at least six inches of water are present. Then wedge sticks into the bottom from the trap, out for a foot, into deep water. This will force the muskrat to swim between the sticks and the bank—where the trap is set.

Set traps by muskrat feed beds. These are spots where muskrats gather to eat. They are identified by fresh root and stem cuttings.

If you can locate the underwater entrance to a muskrat's bank tunnel, this is an excellent location for the body-grip trap.

If trapping when swamps and marshes are frozen, the only sets available will be in muskrat houses. Check your local regulations before setting a trap in or near a muskrat house.

In cold temperatures, be sure to properly seal the house after setting or pulling a trap. First cut a hole in the side of the house with your hatchet. Reach inside and locate the muskrat's dry nest. This is where the trap is set. The trap is wired to a stick propped against the outside of the house. Next take several handfuls of wet vegetation from the interior of the house and set to one side. Put the chunks you chopped loose, when gaining entrance to the house, back in place. Now blob the wet vegetation over these chunks. This will quickly freeze and seal the house, preventing the open water inside from freezing.

Mink

Mink are not as plentiful as muskrat, and they will not tumble to a set if they detect foreign scent at the set location. This makes them tricky to catch in dry-land sets, but it is no great problem to catch them when traps are set underwater. A good procedure after setting a trap for mink in a creek or river is to splash water over the bank and anything else that might retain your scent.

Blind sets are popular for mink. This is setting traps where you believe mink will step. What makes it easy is the mink's habit of investigating every narrow passageway, hole, brush pile, or space under overhanging tree roots along creek, river, or lake shore. If a passageway is too wide, narrow it with weathered sticks or rocks picked off the ground. Wedge them into the creek bottom to narrow a passageway and force the mink to step into your trap. Blind sets come in all shapes and sizes. For example, a hollow log lying in the water with several inches of water running through it, a stump with a hollow between its roots, or a small spring empting into a stream will be investigated by every passing mink. So will trails, holes, or pockets in a stream bank.

Trappers sometimes manufacture their own blind sets. Several weeks before the season opens, build open-ended cubbies along stream banks with a few inches of water running through them. Use logs, rocks, or whatever material is found at the site. These imitate hollow logs, spaces under tree roots, and other natural passageways. You can make open-ended cubbies at home using scrap lumber. These should be six inches high by six inches wide and three feet long. Set these box cubbies out several weeks prior to the trapping season and cover with mud and brush for a natural appearance. No bait or lure is needed.

Another set that will attract mink, and is best made before the season, is the artificial hole set. This is a six-inch-diameter hole dug into the stream bank, angled upward for a foot, and then down, or to one side, so the mink cannot see the end. Such a hole, providing it has had a chance to weather, will incite a mink's curiosity. You can use fish bait or mink lure, but the set is attractive to mink as is. The entrance to the hole can have a few inches of water in it for a wet set, or it can be dug higher along a stream bank and used as a dry-land set. Experienced mink trappers like to have one quarter of their sets dry, should a sudden cold snap put their underwater sets out of commission. Traps set underwater need not be covered. Dry-land sets should be lightly covered with whatever is the natural material at the set location. This might be sand, dirt, leaves, or moss.

Raccoon

Raccoon are relatively easy to trap, but they are confusing at times. They may suddenly leave a stream or lake shore, where they have been making tracks all summer, and head for the hills to raid cornfields and eat wild fruits and nuts that ripen about the time trapping season opens. The smart raccoon trapper combines woodland sets along with streamside sets.

The raccoon is a furbearer actively sought by trappers. (Photo courtesy J. E. Osman, Pennsylvania Game Commission)

Traps set for raccoon can be staked solid, but it is better to have them attached to a drag. This is usually a two-inch-thick length of hardwood tree 10 to 12 feet long. If the trap chain is wired about three feet from one end of the drag, it will act like a spring and prevent the raccoon from getting a solid pull and yanking his foot free. In wooded terrain, a raccoon will not get far before being entangled, and thus be easily found by the trapper.

In woodlands and along fields, trappers can make sets for raccoon in hollow logs, hollow stumps, or build shedlike cubbies with one end left open. The trap is set in the open end, lightly covered, and bait put in the rear. Any kind of fish, even canned sardines, will attract raccoon. If there is a chance of catching farm cats, use sweet baits like honey or peanut butter. Raccoons eat almost anything. Like the black bear, raccoons forage at dumps. These are good set locations.

A large artificial hole dug along a stream bank and then baited is a good set for raccoon. Make it about a foot in diameter and a foot and a half deep, with two inches of water in the entrance in which to set the trap.

Many blind sets will take raccoon. These can be made where the animals enter or exit the water. Raccoons seem particularly fond of large rivers. They frequently den in hollow trees along river bottoms. Simple bait sets will take raccoon. It is not uncommon for a trapper to wedge a stick in the bottom of a stream in shallow water with a slice of apple speared on top and a trap set below. He expects to catch a muskrat but instead finds a valuable raccoon in his trap. When making sets for mink and muskrat, bear in mind the possibility of catching a raccoon and have traps firmly anchored or attached to hardwood drags.

Fox, Coyote, and Wolf

These sly ones are most easily caught early in the fall before snow and freezing and thawing temperatures make life difficult for the trapper. Traps must be treated in a wood-dye solution. The sly canines can detect the odor of steel and rust through a covering of dirt and snow. To avoid leaving human scent at set locations, wear rubber footwear and rubber gloves. These can be periodically sloshed in mud puddles or streams to wash away scents picked up in your car or the roadside. Trappers can further alleviate suspicion by sprinkling a few drops of fox or coyote urine on boot soles and gloves.

Scents, such as blood or animal flesh, attract these animals, but they should be kept off your traps, boots, gloves, etc. Food smells on your trap can cause the quarry to dig up the trap. This usually results in a sprung trap rather than a catch. The only scents you want left at a set location are bait, scent, and urine.

Numerous types of sets will take the sly canines. None is better than the dirt-hole set, which also takes bobcat, raccoon, skunk, opossum, even an occasional mink when made near water. This set imitates another animal's food cache—not unlike a dog burying his bone. Animals like nothing better than to rob the food cache of another, but fear that the animal that buried the food may be lurking nearby. The dirt-hole set should be made out in the open away from high grass, trees, large rocks, and stumps, which could conceal a lurking animal. An ideal location is an unused pasture or stubble field with short grass, and near a woods or marsh that is hunted by foxes or other wild canines. These are easy to find in farming country. In forested terrain, you must follow old logging trails and select a set location within 30 feet of the trail that is fairly open and free of high weeds and undergrowth. Old homestead clearings, abandoned lumber camps, and even broad river sand-bars are also desirable sites.

Making a dirt-hole set is simple. The trick is to make it in the right place and as quickly as possible. The longer you linger the more of your scent will remain. Cut a triangular piece of sod with a small shovel about one foot from corner to corner. Throw this sod into high grass or carry it away with you. But first shake some of the excess dirt into the excavated area. For fox, in one corner of the triangle dig a hole about three inches in diameter and six inches deep. (The hole and excavation should be a little larger for coyote and wolf.) Put this dirt into a one-foot-square dirt-sifter framework of wood having a one-quarter-inch wire mesh across it. The hole should be dug at a 45-degree angle under a small rock or rotted log. This discourages the quarry from digging at the backside of the hole. Now dig a bed for the trap so when set it will be level or slightly below the level of the surrounding dirt. This bed is dug so one edge of the trap will be one inch from the edge of the hole for fox, up to six inches away for coyote and wolf. Before setting a trap, first pound a foot-long hardwood stake into the ground in the center of the trap bed, and slightly below the surface. The fourth link of the trap chain is wired to the stake. A shortened chain makes it impossible for the trapped animal to make high leaps and possibly pull loose. The trap is then set, and dirt that was dug from the hole and placed in the dirt sifter is sifted over the trap to a depth of one-quarter inch.

The final step is to drop one or two pieces of bait into the hole and two or three drops of lure on the edge of the hole. Sprinkle fox urine liberally over the set location and where you have been crouched while making the set.

Part Three

WINTER GAME

ELEVEN

Cottontail

The late-season cottontail is the hardiest of the species, and a real challenge for both hunter and beagles. The weaker rabbits have become victims of weather, hunting, and predators.

Most of our northern forested areas are home to snowshoe hares. Cottontails are confined to farming country in some states. My friend Charlie Mechley, who originally is from Ohio, tells me that raising beagles and chasing cottontails was a way of life in that state. Cottontails are the number-one small-game animal in the United States.

My older brothers and I always thought that if we hunted cottontails late in the season, after there was snow on the ground, there was no danger of contacting tularemia. A medical doctor recently informed me that this is false. Tularemia can be contacted from handling rabbits at any time.

Tularemia is a disease of rabbits, squirrels, etc., caused by a bacterium. It is transmitted to man by insects or by the handling of infected animals. The commonest way to contact tularemia is in field dressing an infected rabbit with an open cut on your hand. This can result in an irregular fever lasting several weeks. It is said to resemble the plague.

Not that we were too concerned. We liked to hunt cottontails after there was plenty of snow on the ground. This made them easier to see, and tracks in the snow indicated the best spots to hunt.

Favorite hunting locations were recently cleared woods, piles of cut firewood, and cleared trees and brush for a fence line. Invariably branch tips would be left heaped in piles. While still fresh, these were very attractive to cottontails. The rabbits fed on the tender branch tips and buds and found refuge under the piles. Here they were safe from foxes and owls, but not from the bloodthirsty little weasel, which is able to penetrate the smallest opening the rabbit can squeeze through.

The rabbits were safe from us if the piles contained stumps, heavy tree limbs, or trunks. It was the brush piles, containing only light branch tips, that gave us action. We were able to rout any rabbit crouched under the pile by getting on top of the pile and jumping up and down. We used shotguns because running shots were the rule. We never knew for sure if a brush pile contained a rabbit, and we often used up a lot of energy on an empty one. We never brought home impressively large numbers of rabbits as is sometimes the case when hunting with hounds. We had to work for every one.

When I say that cottontails are America's number-one small-game animal I should really say that rabbits are number one, because there are many groupings, and not all are called cottontail. Common types include the eastern cottontail, the mountain cottontail, the New

The cottontail rabbit ranks as the number one small-game animal in the United States. (Photo courtesy Charles J. Farmer)

England cottontail, the desert cottontail, the brush rabbit, the marsh rabbit, the swamp rabbit, and the pygmy rabbit. All are generally gray in color, but some are reddish or brownish. They range in size from the tiny pygmy rabbit, 8½ to 11 inches, to the large 17-inch New England cottontail.

The eastern cottontail has the largest range. It extends from New England to the Dakotas and south into Mexico. It is also found in the southern part of the eastern Canadian provinces.

Rabbits are found in every state. The pygmy rabbit is found in Montana, Idaho, Utah, Nevada, California, Oregon, and Washington. The mountain cottontail is found in these same seven states and several more, as well as some Canadian provinces. The eastern cottontail overlaps, to some extent, every group except the pygmy cottontail.

I doubt that one could come up with a favorite or "classic" gun for cottontails. They are taken with every make and model of shotgun and .22 rifle. They are also hunted with pistols, bow and arrow, even slingshots. If using a scattergun, low base loads in No. 6 or No. 7½ shot are effective. Generally, a fairly open choke is called for when hunting cottontails. Improved cylinder is a good choice. But I wouldn't feel terribly handicapped with modified. In the .22 rimfire rifle, the .22 Long Rifle cartridge is a good choice. Most shots at cottontails are close, but it is not unusual to get an occasional long shot. Cottontails like cover, but they will also sit on the very edge of cover, allowing them to be seen from a distance. The .22 Magnum, solid-jacketed bullet, is ideal for the long shots. On numerous occasions while hunting fox in open terrain, I have spotted cottontails sitting along the edge of cover.

Rabbits thrive best in areas containing heavy cover. Such cover may be in the form of brush patches, dense sagebrush, wet areas (marsh and swamp rabbits) with dense cover or briar patches. If you wonder where all the rabbits have gone in your area, it is probably because their brushy habitat is destroyed. Predators take many rabbits. If there is sufficient brush, however, the reproductive rate of bunnies will keep ahead of birds of prey and other predators.

Rabbits are very adaptable, especially the common eastern cottontail. It can find food and shelter in an overgrown city dump almost as well as in brushy forest areas, and is especially fond of edges or border areas, such as a weed-choked ditch, brushy fencerow, and hedge. A woodlot that had been cut to the ground provided me with several years of rifle shooting at cottontails.

Winter cottontails should be hunted during the high-sun part of the day, because they won't stray far from their holes when the temperature drops to 20 degrees or under. Cottontails will sometimes hold tight in a sunny spot until almost stepped on. This makes them as much a target for the rifleman as for the shotgun hunter.

Out Wyoming way, outdoor writer Charlie Farmer hunts three kinds of rabbit: eastern cottontail, mountain cottontail, and desert cottontail. "The Bighorn basin," he says, "is the late-season leader. The season extends from August through March. December and January are good bets when other seasons close and before coyotes and long winter take their toll of bunnies. The area around Medicine Bow is also good prospect. Sagebrush plains, near rock outcroppings around Cody, provide fast, late-season gunning."

The beagle is the only breed worth considering when it comes to chasing cottontails with hounds. You can hunt cottontails with a single hound or with a dozen. A strong desire to hunt is a characteristic that every hunter looks for in a prospective beagle. Sometimes these over-eager hounds are a headache to round up at day's end.

Most prefer a hound with a melodious voice, one that

Distribution Range of Cottontail

Western cottontails like to sit in sun on cold winter days. They're never far from a hole, and a .22 is the best medicine. (Photo courtesy Jim Zumbo)

opens up well on a warm trail but is not so mouthy as to be constantly barking, even on a cold trail.

A good nose is obviously desirable, especially if you are hunting with only a single hound. In a large pack, a poor nose or two can take their lead from the others and add to the music.

Some experienced hound men prefer female hounds.

The female, they believe, is more even-tempered and manageable. Some will even say the female is more alert, more intelligent, yet aggressive enough for the job. Beagles, male or female, are friendly dogs that make good house pets as well as hunters. It is no trick to spoil one. A young hound on first encountering a stream or ditch may whine asking for help across. Give the hound that help and he expects it from then on. Sometimes a little shove will get the dog started.

Cottontails tend to circle, which makes them ideal for chasing with hounds. The hunter generally finds a stump or other elevated view near where the cottontail was jumped and waits for it to circle back. If there is snow, you can see where hound and rabbit have crossed an opening, and wait there for their possible return. When hunters chase rabbits in the same area for many years, they usually become more proficient at intercepting the quarry. Cottontails jumped from a certain weed patch will often use the same escape route year after year. Certain crossings become fabled hot spots.

Hunting cottontails with hounds is the most efficient means of hunting them, but more often the cottontail is hunted by one or two hunters without dogs. In the case of two hunters, one might carry a 12-gauge automatic and leftover duck loads, while the other is armed with a pistol chambered for .22 rimfire. The hunter with the shotgun can work more swiftly through prospective cover. If he flushes a rabbit he can take the bunny on the run. The hunter with the pistol (or rifle) will have to work more slowly. When a concentration of tracks and trails is located, he must circle, zigzag, and generally cover the location thoroughly. Remember that cottontails will often hold still and allow the hunter to walk on by.

Hunting with beagle hounds provided these Tennessee hunters with plenty of action. (Photo courtesy Carlos Vinson)

If you locate a rabbit's form (bed), you have a good chance of locating the rabbit. These are easy to identify in snow. Without snow, look for a small, oval patch of crushed weeds and grass. Chances are the rabbit is sitting nearby in another form. Mark the spot with your cap or hang a handkerchief above the spot. Then work

A high vantage point is good for intercepting fast-stepping rabbits ahead of hounds.

your way away from the form in small circles, returning each time to the form. It's a good bet that the rabbit will be within 30 or 40 yards of the form. By systematically working from the old form in every direction, you can locate the rabbit. Look for forms off to the side of well used rabbit trails. Walk a zigzag pattern to the left and to the right of the trail.

A popular outfit for rabbits is the .22-410 combination rifle and shotgun. The rifle barrel is used for the sitting shots and the shotgun barrel on the running shots. If I was thinking in terms of a shotgun only for rabbits, I would lean toward a lightweight 20 gauge. I like a scopesight when hunting with the .22 rifle. A 4X scope is about right, and helps spot rabbits at a distance. This is particularly true if you use a scope designed for use on a big-game rifle. It provides much greater light-gathering power and the resulting increased visibility.

Rabbits blend in remarkably well. I try for head shots only. This is no big feat, since a rabbit's head is almost as generous a target as its chest area. Frequently the rabbit's head is seen first because of its shiny black eye.

As with other small-game animals and birds, I like to field dress rabbits on the spot. This ensures good eating and makes the final cleaning job at home that much easier. You can also do a complete cleaning job in the field. Bring along plastic bags and store the dressed and skinned rabbits in these bags. When you get home the already packaged meat can go directly into the freezer. Some hunters will cut the rabbit in half, keeping the lower portion—the hind legs and lower back—since about 90 percent of the eating meat is in this part of the rabbit. I have done this with snowshoe hares for many years.

The eastern cottontail, with which I am most familiar, is one of the finest-eating small game. Simmered in water and then lightly fried, it is always a treat. The meat is light in color and tender. You can also take a chance on making Hasenpfeffer. The last time I tried I spoiled it with too much vinegar. The following recipe is a good one, but go easy on the vinegar:

Wash and clean the rabbit, and cut into serving pieces. Soak in water to cover, to which one-half cup vinegar has been added. Let stand overnight, drain, and put the meat in a deep crock. Cover with equal parts of water and vinegar, add one slice of lemon, four cloves, two bay leaves, one teaspoon salt, one-half teaspoon peppercorns.

Let the meat soak in the liquid for at least two days. Drain the meat, brown thoroughly in butter, turning often, and gradually add the marinade. Simmer for forty minutes. Stir in one cup sour cream and simmer an additional ten minutes. Pour back into the crock. This will keep for one week to ten days. Heat as much as you want to use each time.

TWELVE

Snowshoe Hare

The snowshoe is a true hare, but the name rabbit rolls off the tongue easier and in most areas of its range they are called snowshoe rabbits, or simply snowshoes. If you want to get technical, the proper name is "varying hare." The snowshoe is white in winter, dark brown in summer. I have both in my backyard. In summer the snowshoe's brown is distinguishable from the cotton-tail's gray. The cottontail will eat from my garden, the snowshoe won't. It is interesting to watch the snow-shoes change color as winter approaches. Their feet, ears, and stomach are the first to grow winter white fur. Next comes a palomino shade. This, I think, makes them look like domestic rabbits. Finally, only a little grayish-brown lines the center of their backs and crosses the top of the head and face.

The snowshoe is small compared to other hares and jackrabbits, but bigger than most cottontails, and will weigh from two to four pounds. It has large hind feet that enables it to move about in deep snow; the softer

157

the snow, the more enlarged will be the snowshoe's snowshoelike track.

Snowshoes are found all across the northern tier of states, extending southward into the Appalachian Mountains, Rocky Mountains, and California high country. They are found throughout Canada and Alaska. Snowshoes are a ready source of protein for many predators.

Twig ends and buds are the two main foodstuffs of snowshoes in winter. They also eat a great deal of bark from the trunks of poplar and alder saplings. I used to hear that snowshoes were not fit to eat in late winter because of this heavy diet of bark. Not so. Snowshoes taken in late February are as tasty as those taken in fall and early winter.

The snowshoe hare population will run in cycles. But even when numbers are high, good hunting depends on finding good habitat. The snowshoe cannot exist in open, parklike woods. Logging and controlled burning, which are so beneficial in promoting lush new second-growth and increased habitat for deer and grouse, are equally good for snowshoes.

Rifles and shotguns used for snowshoes are as varied as they are for cottontails. Pistols and .22 rifles are more commonly used because it is hard to budge a snowshoe when he's convinced he is concealed.

I use a .22 rifle for hunting snowshoes. I have used a shotgun and I would often bag every bunny seen when I hunted with the scattergun. Now as many as half will escape by running. It is close to impossible to take them on the run with a rifle in the thick brush they frequent. Using a rifle forces me to hunt quietly and spot my quarry on the site. Shotguns would be appropriate when hunting with hounds and the big bunnies are kept moving.

My favorite spots for hunting snowshoes are thickets of second-growth aspen (popple). These are where logging, or sometimes fire, has taken place. Most of the stands we hunt are around ten to fifteen years old. The trees are rarely more than 20 feet tall or more than three or four inches in diameter.

Look for them in willow and alder swamps, in low lands of spruce and cedar, in thickets of hazel brush and sumac, in tangles of any kind bordering pine plantations. When the going gets tough and you have to thread your way through junglelike tangles, you're in snowshoe country.

Snowshoes are difficult to get near when the snow is crusted and noisy. In soft snow the hunter can sometimes walk within two or three feet of a snowshoe, fully in view all the way, providing he does so quietly. An exception to this is when the snowshoe runs from its bed. If the snowshoe stops within view, the hunter must immediately take a shot from where he stands; any further movement will cause the snowshoe to bolt.

A snowshoe jumped from its bed can be tracked down and shot in fresh snow. But it's not always easy. Once its thoroughly alerted the not-too-brainy snowshoe becomes a difficult quarry.

The snowshoe hare has a great affinity for edges. In the roadside woods I hunt, I first work the wood's edge bordering the roadside. Next I walk old logging trails or ditch banks running through the woods. I work the edges of clearings, swamps, creeks, and trails. Only then do I dive into the heart of the woods.

I've been hunting snowshoe hares for eight or nine

The author with a brace of snowshoe hares.

The author hunting snowshoes in abandoned open-pit mine. Light cover here makes the hares easier to locate.

years and have enjoyed every hunt, even the tough ones in thigh-deep snow and bitter cold. What he lacks in brain power the snowshoe hare more than makes up for in being a tough bunny to see.

I wasn't too thrilled with my first meal or two of snowshoe hare. The dark meat was not as mild as cotton-

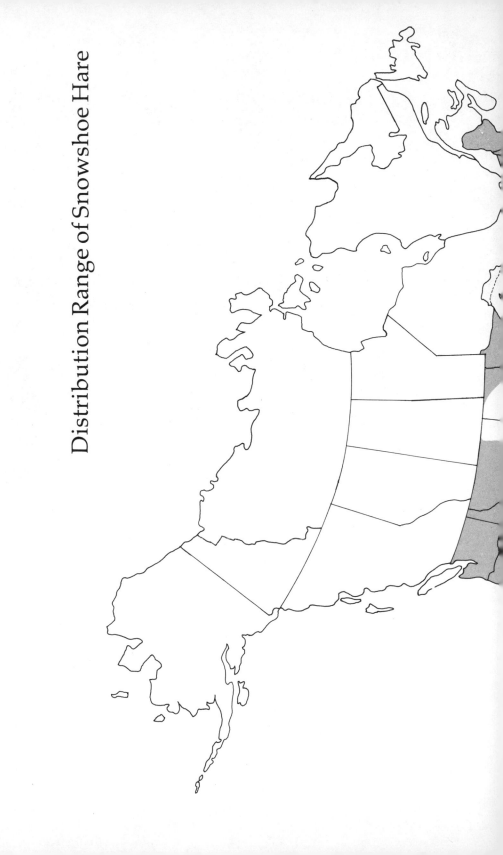

Distribution Range of Snowshoe Hare

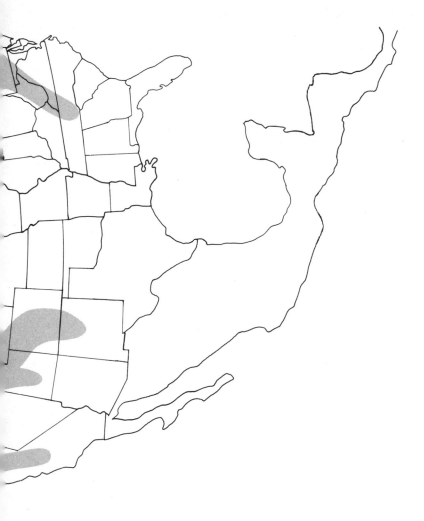

tail or squirrel. The long leg bones turned off the more squeamish members of my family. Finally, I tried deboning the meat, filleting from each hind leg the meat from the upper thigh, and two long slices paralleling the lower backbone. I cut these into bite-size pieces, and was on my way to good eating.

Soak the choice pieces in salt water for an hour. Then put the pieces in a deep pan with a quarter-inch of water. Put on a cover and let simmer for half-an-hour at low heat. Toward the end of this time, add a half-cup of barbecue sauce. Then remove the cover so steam can escape and the water boil down. When the meat is lightly browned it is ready to serve. It goes well with fried potatoes and cold beer.

THIRTEEN

Jackrabbit

When I lived near good jackrabbit country and before I became addicted to hunting fox and other predators, jackrabbits embarrassed me on a regular basis. But I hit enough of them to gain confidence in my ability to take game on the run with a rifle. I know of no other animal that provides such a variety of shooting situations and exists in such great numbers as the jackrabbits of North America.

They are many things to many people. For outdoor writer Sam Fadala, who was raised in Arizona, the jackrabbit was all things during his boyhood: substitute for big game; teacher of fast-running shooting; something to find with binoculars as they blended with the desert in their bedding sites, and, in the case of young jacks, a source of good food. (Sam's Italian grandmother used the hindquarters in spaghetti sauce.) These were the black-tailed and possibly the antelope jackrabbit. Later he hunted the white-tailed jackrabbit in Canada. These are the three jackrabbits of North America.

This hunter wears snowshoes to find snowshoe hares in high country. (Photo courtesy Jim Zumbo)

The antelope jackrabbit has huge, seven- to eight-inch ears, and a very small head. His general coloration is gray with a whitish cast along the sides and hips. His home is Mexico but his range extends into Arizona.

The black-tailed jackrabbit is common throughout the West and in Mexico. The white-tailed jackrabbit is found where the blacktail is shy in numbers in the

All winter hunting isn't snow and cold. This jackrabbit was photographed in southwestern Arizona desert in December. (Photo courtesy William Curtis)

northern states of Montana and the Dakotas. The white-tailed jackrabbit ranges across southern British Columbia, Alberta, Saskatchewan, and Manitoba. He is found from Wisconsin to Washington and south to New Mexico.

When shotguns are used for jackrabbit hunting, high-

Distribution Range of Jackrabbit

base loads in No. 2 and No. 4 shot are good choices in a full-choke barrel. The .22 rimfire rifles, particularly automatics, are popular for jackrabbit hunting.My older brother Jim used to occasionally bowl one over with a .22 pistol. The rimfires are a bit light, however. Better are the hot centerfire 22s, the .22-250, .222, .223, etc. In the really wide open spaces of the West you can use the excellent .24 and .25 calibers; the .243, 6mm, .25-06— even the heavier .270 and .30-06. There is no better practice for the big-game hunter than to use his heavy artillery on jacks. Some of these cannons make quite a racket, but with a little common sense they can be used safely.

Farming and ranching practices, as well as predators and disease, all have their effects on jackrabbit populations. I remember in 1951 we had fantastic numbers of jackrabbits in the southern and western counties of Minnesota. The following year their numbers dropped and fox numbers multiplied. Now with fox numbers thinning because of high prices for their pelts, I expect that jackrabbit numbers will again multiply. But there are many contributing components, not the least of which are insecticides and other chemicals. Mysterious population cycles are common with hares and rabbits.

Whitetail jacks turn all white in the winter and are often mistaken for snowshoe hares, but are much larger. Whitetails prefer large open-type farms with big stubble fields. Winter wheat fields are favored habitats. Look for them at elevations of between 6,000 and 8,000 feet. Best hunting techniques include walking along edges of cover next to stubble fields and brushy benches or draws in proximity to the fields. Shotguns are effective, but riflemen have great shooting opportunities at the fast-stepping hares. A fun method is to track jacks after a fresh snowfall. Patience and perseverance will ultimately lead the hunter to the quarry, although a whitetail can make several miles of tracks in one evening. They are strictly nocturnal and are seldom seen in daytime. Sitting shots are rare, since they bed down around cover and secrete themselves.

Blacktails retain their gray color throughout the winter. They are more common than whitetails and are especially plentiful in big expanses of sagebrush. Elevations of 5,000 to 7,000 feet produce the kind of habitat that blacktails like. Best hunting procedure is to walk slowly through sagebrush and flush bedded hares. This kind of hunting lends itself well to large numbers of hunters. Gunners should spread out 25 yards apart and walk slowly through the sage. It is imperative, however, to exercise extreme caution when shooting at the speedy hares. Blacktail populations fluctuate according to a regular cycle regardless of hunting pressure. Their numbers are controlled by disease and predators (primarily coyotes). Although most wildlife species exhibit this cyclic fluctuation, blacktails show perhaps the greatest changes in numbers.

The top time to find winter jackrabbits, in warmer climates, is the morning after a good rain. The jacks leave their soaked brush or grass hideouts and seek open sunny spots.

I always found the scope-sighted varmint rifle to be ideal for hunting jacks. The shots are often long ones, and for its size, the jack is a tough animal to put down. I still have a small snapshot of the first jackrabbit I shot with a varmint rifle. I no longer recall the model number of the rifle, but it was a Winchester bolt action chambered for the .218 Bee cartridge. A rather light, wind-sensitive bullet, the .218, with factory ammo, was effective to about 150 yards. I'd bought it the summer before.

I was hunting with one of my brothers west of the Twin Cities, Minneapolis and St. Paul. My brother walked in another direction while I followed the contours of a shallow ravine. I walked along the top of the ravine near one edge. It was about 70 yards across to the other side. There were scattered clumps of bushes in the ravine and the snow was laced with jackrabbit tracks and trails.

Suddenly a big jack burst from under cover and with outlandish bounds headed up the opposite side of the ravine. I dropped to a sitting position and followed the jack through the 4-power scopesight. When he reached the top, the jack stopped and stood on the toes of his hind feet for a closer look at what had disturbed him. It was a last look that cost him dearly.

When there is little snow, jacks will often lie in the furrows of plowed fields. Unless you are hunting with a large party, this can be tough hunting, especially if the fields roll on and on. Jacks like to be out of the winter wind but will not necessarily seek shelter on the extreme leeward side of a hill to escape it. A shallow depression, most anywhere in a plowed field, will serve. Look for the roughest plowed fields for the best action. Pay particular attention to the edges near cover.

Late in the winter when the snow lies deep is the best time for the lone hunter, or one or two hunters, to hunt the white-tailed jackrabbit with varmint rifles. Deep snow of a foot or more narrows the possibilities where a jack will bed down. A jack will rarely go underground, preferring to form a depression in the snow or dig a short tunnel into a snowdrift. Here he lies with his nose near the opening.

Old gravel pits are favorite bedding sites. Jacks can

Dave Colby notes jackrabbit tracks along fence line cover.

find shelter here no matter how the four winds blow.

Drifts along snow fences are another favorite bedding site when the snow lies deep. Jacks will dig tunnels into these snowdrifts. I remember once Jim and I could see a jack lying in one of these snow tunnels. We spotted him from the road. Jim drove the car ahead until we were out of sight. Then we quickly put on snowshoes and hurried up and over the embankment and walked back to where we came out by the snow fence and right in front of the jack's nose.

When he came out of his tunnel, the jack's ears laid flat against the sides of his head. He was moving so fast he didn't hop, just streaked low across the snow.

Dave Colby carries out a hefty white-tailed jackrabbit.

When we find a field, under deep snow conditions, where tracks indicate jackrabbits have been feeding, we take a long look around. Chances are the jacks will not be lying in the same field but will be bedded on one of the surrounding hillsides. Look for old pieces of farm machinery protruding out of the snow; jacks will burrow into the snow on the leeward side of these. Look for woodlots that have isolated clumps of bushes running out from them; jacks like to camp under these. Bushes growing along fence lines are good too.

174

The best spot of all is a willow swamp. Not a really big swamp. These are too difficult to hunt. The best are the size of one or two city lots, or sometimes only the size of a living-room floor. If there are any jacks in the nearby countryside, these clumps of willows will be interlaced with tracks and trails.

While a spot like this is always worth walking out to, you can also find them right alongside country roads and highways. An important point to remember is that these are tough spots to hunt alone. Invariably the jack or jacks will run out the opposite side of the willows from where you walked in. A good setup is to have one or two companions off to the sides and slightly ahead of the driver.

Can you trail a jack if you miss him? You bet. But don't be surprised if you find you are on the trail of a pretty smart hombre. I've had easier times trailing foxes.

A favorite ruse of the jackrabbit is to run in a well-traveled trail in the snow, and then make a tremendous leap off to one side in an effort to throw you off his track. A jack will pick a high vantage point and watch his own backtrail. At the first sight of you he's long gone. But stay with him. Sooner or later he will bed down in a spot where you will be able to get within range before he jumps.

Neophytes invariably overestimate the size of jackrabbits. Without blinking an eye, I have heard men describe shooting jacks that weighed 15 pounds or better. They don't grow that big. For several winters I made it a practice to check the weights of white-tailed jackrabbits we killed. The average was about 6¾ pounds. This was in the winter when they are at their heaviest. A few old gray-faced animals pulled the scales up to the 7½-pound mark.

I would like to report that jackrabbits are delicious. But they're not. Edible, yes. But not really what I would call good eating. I remember once my mother served up two big platters of rabbit. One platter was cottontail the other jackrabbit. The platter of cottontail was wiped clean, but only a few of the braver souls cared to chew on the tough, dark meat of the jackrabbit.

If I were to cook jackrabbit today, I would undoubtedly follow the same procedure I use with snowshoe hares, that of filleting the meat from the bones and cutting into bite-size pieces.

FOURTEEN

Fox

The red fox is about the size of a small dog, colored reddish with hints of black on the upper parts, white underneath, with blackish lower legs and feet. Ears are pointed, and stand erect. He has a white-tipped tail. The silver, cross, black, etc., are color phases of the red and carry the same characteristics. The red fox averages 8 to 14 pounds.

The gray fox is a grizzled gray on the upper parts, white to ash-gray underneath with hints of orange. The tip of his tail is dark gray to black. The gray fox averages 7 to 11 pounds.

The kit fox, also called desert or swift fox, is a yellowish-gray on the upper parts, similarly colored underneath except for a white throat patch. He has a black-tipped tail. The kit fox can be readily recognized by his very long ears. The kit fox averages 4 to 5½ pounds.

The Arctic fox is, in summer, brownish to slate on the upper parts, yellowish white underneath. In the winter

The red fox. This sly canine is available to hunters all across North America. There are many ways to hunt him.

he is white or slate blue on both the upper parts and underneath. His tail tip matches his body color summer and winter. The Arctic fox averages 7 to 15 pounds.

The red fox is the most widespread of the foxes. With the exception of parts of the extreme Southeast, Southwest, and Plains states, he is found throughout most of North America. The gray fox fills in some of the gaps where the red fox is not found. The gray fox is found in the Southwest and throughout all of the entire eastern United States.

The little kit fox is found in the Southwest and the Plains along the eastern edge of the Rockies.

The Arctic fox is found in the extreme northern reaches of Alaska and Canada.

The red and gray foxes are the two primary targets of hunters. The red fox prefers the more open farmlands, while the gray fox is at home in heavier undergrowth of briars, scrub oaks, laurel and rhododendron swamps. The gray fox is one up on the red fox; the gray fox can climb trees. His feet, however, do not have the protective tufts of fur between the pads as do those of the red fox. This is probably a disadvantage in ice and snow. Some areas will hold equal numbers of both red foxes and gray foxes. In other areas, the gray fox is confined to a few areas of heavy growth and river bottom and the red fox predominates in more open farmland. In areas where the cover is more suitable to gray fox, the gray fox may drive out what red foxes are in the area. Red foxes are afraid of the scrappy gray fox.

Rifles and shotguns suitable for fox are many and varied. Shotguns are often used when pursuing foxes with hounds or when a group of hunters make drives. They are particularly useful for close-range work, as in hunting gray foxes in woodlots. They have the advantage of doing minimum damage to the animal's fur. High-base loads of No. 2 shot in 12 gauge will kill a fox at 40 yards.

A well-placed shot with a .22 rimfire rifle or pistol will kill a fox. However, getting close enough to make an

Distribution Range of Red Fox

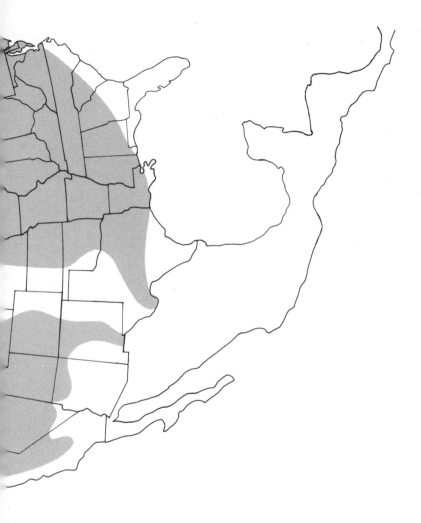

Distribution Range of Gray Fox

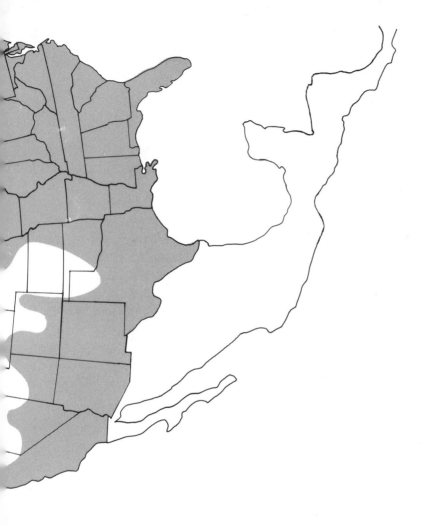

accurate shot with such relatively short-range weapons doesn't happen often. More efficient are the hot center-fire .22s. Even then, a poorly placed shot will result in a wounded fox. Foxes are very tenacious of life. You can hunt them with your favorite deer rifle, too. But only the more accurate calibers should be used, and then only in areas where they can be used safely.

Some popular cartridges for fox include the .222, .223, .225, .243, .25-06, .257 Roberts, .264, and .270.

Because predator pelts sometimes command high prices, hunters who handload are experimenting with loads that do minimum damage to the fur. But with a gaping bullet hole, all is not lost. You can repair the damage by sewing the hole in the pelt closed before drying it. This sounds unethical, but many fur buyers recommend it and will in turn give you a higher price for the pelt.

The gray fox is considered easier to hunt with hounds than the red fox. Because the red fox prefers more open habitat he gives the hunter with hounds a more exciting chase. The gray fox will frequently tree after a relatively short chase. But he does have a bag of tricks that includes zigzagging back and forth in the thickest, most impenetrable cover he can find. By the time the hounds unravel the trail he has made another erratic route in another thicket.

The clever red fox will take to a wooden fence when being pursued and hop from fence post to fence post, or from rock to rock along a stone wall to break up his trail. He doubles back, and will even show himself to his pursuers as if to tease them. There is the often told story of the red fox who was chased to the edge of a cliff by seven hounds. He stopped on the very brink and stood in front of a cluster of low bushes that concealed the

This fox was sighted hunting during midday. Foxes will often hunt during a snowfall.

edge. He waited as if accepting defeat. Then at the last moment, with the hounds rushing forward, he scooted to one side and all seven hounds plunged to their death.

You don't need a lot of people or hounds to hunt foxes. The hunter who owns several Triggs, Walker, or other breed of foxhound can hunt on his own. Snow will help the hunter locate fresh tracks. Over the years the hunter will become more familiar with his hunting territory and will learn favorite runways and crossings used by fox.

The gray fox is fairly easy to deceive with a predator call. Easy, that is, if you have taken the time and made the effort to learn his habits and characteristics. Above all, you must give your predator call a fair chance. Hunters frequently feel foolish the first few times they try blowing a predator call. Many who try it give up after making one or two stands. One approach is to first spend a day scouting for fresh signs—tracks, trails, droppings, etc.—and looking for good calling sites. Look for spots near a fresh sign that will force the gray fox to cross a small clearing as he responds to your call. Have a tree or wood pile or other natural backing picked out to hunker down by as you call. Early the following morning, and again that afternoon, you can approach the selected sites without any fuss. The sound of your call will not carry far in wooded terrain, and you will not have to move more than 500 yards between calling sites.

Calling red foxes is more difficult. It is best to call while in an open field or other exposed spot, because the red fox is reluctant to approach cover in answering a call. Lying prone is one way of staying out of sight in open terrain. If there is snow, wear white or cover yourself with a white sheet. Carry a sheet of tough plastic to lie on. Sometimes you can find cover along a fence line. The more open the country, the more out in the open you should try to be. Where red foxes are living in fairly wooded terrain, you can sometimes crouch down against a log or brush pile.

Most of my fox hunting has been limited to hunting red foxes in open farm country without the use of dogs or predator calls. The idea on these hunts is to try to spot the fox sleeping and then take a shot or stalk within range. A novice once asked me if this wasn't unsporting; shooting a fox in his bed. The fact is there is nothing more difficult.

Not all foxes are seen sleeping. Often the fox sees me first and is up and running. At other times I intercept foxes hunting during midday. Sometimes the fox will be lying in heavy grass or down in a cattail swamp and my first glimpse of the animal will be of his tail floating over a hilltop. But I always watch for sleeping foxes. I do this by carefully glassing each new leeward slope as it comes into view, also log piles, fenceline snowdrifts, haystacks, ditch banks, and the entrances to dens. The important thing is to always look as far ahead as possible. If you do not see a fox sleeping, at least you will see him run.

With increased snowmobile activity this method is becoming less effective. It can still be done, however, and the more experienced you become the better you get at seeing this sly canine before he sees you. Look for a furry ball. The red fox will curl up like a dog with the tip of his nose under the tip of his tail. This furry ball will appear about one foot in diameter and have a soft outline. Rocks and frozen clods of dirt have hard, clearly defined outlines. In good light the red fox may appear as red as he really is, but not always. He can look brown, even black, from a distance. Look for his black-tipped ears. If still in doubt, just sit and wait. Rarely will ten

Norman Johnson is awaiting a fox after making a call along a fence line. In 1971 Norm bagged 55 foxes. (Photo courtesy Norman Johnson)

minutes pass without the fox raising his head for a look at the surrounding terrain.

If you miss the shot, do not despair. You can track

him down and get another shot. There was a time, back when my brothers and I first started hunting foxes, when trailing a fox was a matter of following his tracks over one or two hills and there he would be, fast asleep again on the next slope. The winter scene is a lot more crowded nowadays, and foxes are used to being trailed or even chased, so you may be in for an all-day tracking job. It could be your most memorable hunt.

"In general," reports Norman Johnson, "female foxes will stay year after year in the area where they were born, while the young male foxes migrate out of the area, usually the following winter about February. Female foxes den up more readily than do the male foxes, especially in late winter after mating. A fox scared into a den will often emerge immediately after the danger has passed. By habit, foxes use the same crossings from one area to another, and will lie in the same general area to sleep. Male foxes are more easily caught by fur trappers, leaving a high percentage of female foxes to go through the winter, often bearing no young, as foxes normally mate for life. Foxes will cover five to six miles each night, if walking is not too difficult. They often stay for a few days in heavy sheltered areas after a heavy snow. Foxes like to spend the day in large, weedy ravines, particularly if a den is nearby. If one fox is shot in such an area, another will take his place either that year or another year. A good fox area will attract foxes almost to the exact sleeping place year after year, it's just a foxy place. In the winter foxes will bed down by or near a den. They love to lie in the sun, away from the wind. Don't pursue a wounded fox too quickly. If they are allowed to lie down a few minutes they will be easier to stalk. A wounded fox, even badly hit, has amazing stamina.

"Foxes," Norm continues, "sleep most soundly between the hours of 10:00 A.M. and 3:30 P.M. Foxes often wait until dark to get up from their bed, but usually get up just before dark. February foxes get up much earlier, as the day is longer and they get hungry before dark, and at this time of year food is scarce and will cause them to start searching for food earlier. Foxes usually mate in mid-January through the first part of February. Foxes will select a mate quite some time before the mating season and can be found lying together even in December. The habits of the red fox are consistent but will vary with conditions. Foxes which normally lie in the wide open fields each day will not do this in areas frequented by noisy snowmobiles. Foxes hunted heavily by hounds, guns, traps, etc., will take to cover more quickly than foxes left alone. These foxes will come out later in the evening and duck in just as early in the morning before hunters are out. Foxes quickly become familiar with danger and obviate the conditions which may cost them their lives. Because of their ability to adjust, we will always have foxes around."

FIFTEEN

Bobcat and Coyote

Like all cats, the bobcat is built for killing and will range over a lot of country to satisfy his hunger. The bobcat is predominantly gray, although he may have an almost reddish tone to his coat, with dark spots or blotches around his belly and legs. These are more prominent on younger animals. He has a short "bobtail" white-tipped and weighs from 12 to 45 pounds. The coat of the bobcat is generally more mottled than that of the Canadian lynx.

The bobcat is found from southern Canada throughout the entire United States and south into Mexico. He is very rare in the Plains States. He is far more able to live near man than is his northern cousin the lynx.

Bobcat are found in different environments and are also omnivorous, eating everything they can catch. Bobcats are extremely secretive and are seldom seen. They bed down in thickets and brushy draws. In winter they like to hunt along southern exposures because they don't care to travel in snow, and south faces offer dry

Dennis Seline, a Minnesota hunter, leads his hound to a fresh bobcat track.

footing. Cottontail are favored prey. Varmint calling is the best way to hunt bobcats unless hounds are available. In the winter, after a snowfall, the best technique is to take the dogs to an area popular with bobcats. After a fresh track is found, turn the dogs loose and prepare for a long chase. Although cats don't have lungs capable of sustaining long chases, they'll pull plenty of tricks to keep the dogs on their toes.

An old single shot in 12 gauge is a good choice for winter bobcat hunting with hounds. Shotguns get rough abuse riding on a snowmobile to the hunting area or when the hunter is pushing his way through an alder swamp on snowshoes. You rarely get more than one shot at a bobcat running ahead of hounds. High base loads in No. 2 shot is a good choice in factory ammo. Dennis Seline uses a Winchester Model 37A single shot, firing handloaded 3-inch Magnums. He believes the strong action of a single shot gives a safety margin and he overloads his shells with 35 grains of A.L. 7 behind a plastic shot cup packed with 1⅝ ounces of Winchester copper-plated No. 2 shot. Rifles, except .22 rimfires, are generally discouraged because they damage the bobcat's fur.

Coyotes are ubiquitous. There is no habitat they cannot survive in. For example, their population is increasing within the city limits of Los Angeles. Early winter produces the best hunting because the young coyotes are somewhat naive and have not yet learned the facts of life. They become educated in a hurry, however, and have earned a degree once they've been spooked by a hunter.

The coyote is uniformly grizzled-gray in color and weighs from 20 to 50 pounds. He is, essentially, a wolf in a small package. While the timber wolf is losing ground, the coyote is extending his range. They are found in significant numbers in almost every state west of the Mississippi, and east of the Mississippi in Wis-

Distribution Range of Bobcat

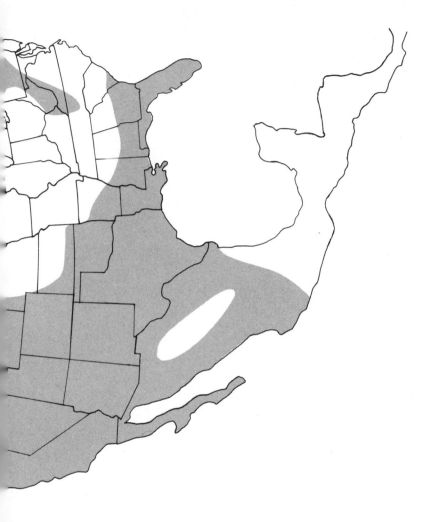

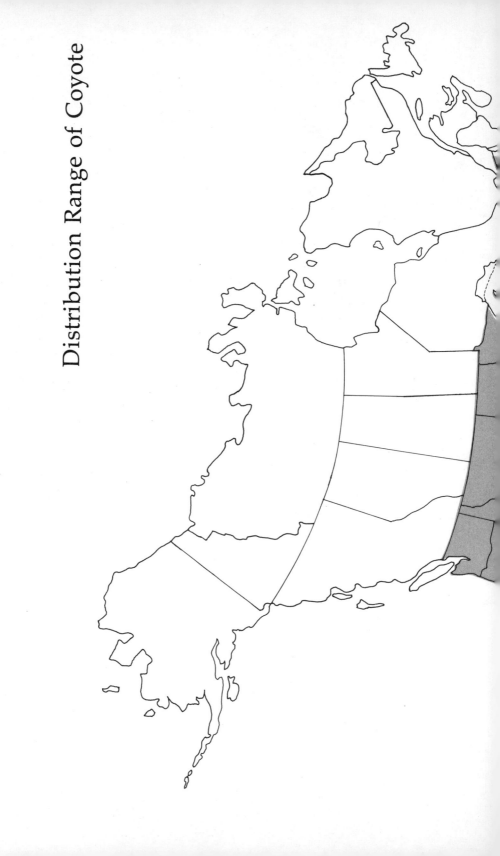

Distribution Range of Coyote

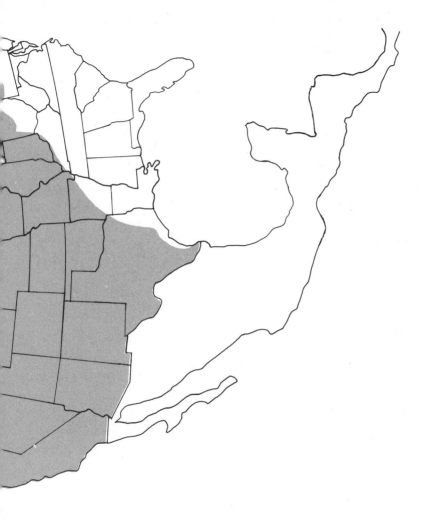

197

consin, Michigan, Illinois, and Indiana. They are reported in many of the easternmost states, and are now well established in the Adirondacks. In Canada, only the easternmost provinces are free of coyotes. They are well established in Alaska but did not exist there until about 1900.

Look for coyotes where there is a plentiful food supply. Areas that support high rabbit and hare populations are good. Tracks in the snow should indicate population densities, since coyotes move many miles in search for food. Don't overlook spots that seem barren and devoid of life. Desert areas that grow only sparse plants often support plenty of coyotes; mice make up a big part of their diet and are found there.

Calling with a predator call is almost the exclusive way to hunt coyotes, but there is an interesting variation. In the winter, coyotes are hard pressed for food and are always looking for a big hearty meal. A carcass of a large animal is perfect, and coyotes will return to the carcass every evening until it is reduced to a few bones. Hunters who discover winter-killed deer, elk, or livestock can utilize the carcass if coyotes are eating from it. Take a stand 100 yards or so away from the carcass, where you can watch the area. Enter your vantage point so coyotes entering the area won't cross your tracks. Keep watch of the wind. Chances are good that coyotes will approach the meat before dark. If an evening stand doesn't work, try the same method in the morning, but be sure to get there at first light.

Some of the men I hunt bobcats with in northern Minnesota also chase brush wolves (coyotes) with their hounds. They prefer to do this in areas having many roads. The coyote is long-winded and is less inclined to circle than the bobcat. Where there are many roads the

Russell Tinsley hefts a big coyote he shot in Colorado. (Photo courtesy Russell Tinsley)

hunters have a better chance of getting ahead of coyote and hounds. Shotguns are used for this type of hunting, but so are centerfire rifles, because shots may be long.

Coyotes are also taken by riflemen in the open country of the West, by walking into country frequented by coyotes and watching for the animals with the aid of binoculars. As in hunting foxes, it is possible to spot the coyote in his bed. The hunter also has a chance of jumping a coyote from cover or intercepting one hunting in daylight.

In some areas of the West, coyotes will sleep during the day in rocky ledges on mountain slopes. At night they descend to the lowlands to hunt, returning to the high ledges at daylight. A little checking after a snowfall will serve to show the routes used most often. The hunter can select an ambush point, and by arriving at this point well before daylight ambush coyotes returning to their daylight bedding sites.

Pinpoint accuracy is required of the rifleman. Some popular loads for coyote include the .222, .223, .225, .243, 6 mm, .25-06, .257, .264, .270, and .30-06.

Luring in coyotes with a predator call requires that the animals be within range of the caller. Some hunters are now locating coyotes by "bugling." It is, Jim Zumbo tells me, the newest wrinkle in predator calling, and is spreading rapidly throughout the Rocky Mountain states.

The obvious advantage of bugling for coyotes, he says, is that it makes so-called "blind calling" unnecessary. The hunter blows the bugle and determines the presence of the animal by listening for a coyote to howl back. Then he figures the animal's approximate location and moves into the correct position. By knowing where the coyotes are, the caller can utilize the terrain to his best advantage and move in accordance with the wind. Much time is saved by not having to call in areas where coyotes are absent.

Some of these bugles are fashioned from old automobile horns. By inserting a reed from an ordinary duck call into the horn stem and blowing it like a trumpet, a

By blowing on a makeshift bugle, this hunter is able to lure coyotes into howling. Once you have coyotes pinpointed, bringing them in with a regular coyote call is easier. (Photo courtesy Jim Zumbo)

high, shrill tone can be created. Bugle enthusiasts claim that the noise created by their horns carries much farther than predator calls. According to coyote buglers, the shriller tones are the most desirable. Conservation officers and game wardens have long known that a coyote will respond to a siren. The new electronic-type sirens that wail and warble at exceedingly high key seem to work best. These sirens can be flipped off instantly, unlike the conventional type that must run down slowly, thus making it difficult to hear a coyote respond.

However you seek him, the coyote is one of the most cunning and tough animals to hunt. He is a superb hunter and can run all day if he has to. He has a keen nose and eyesight second to none. He can change direc-

By using both a shotgun and rifle, these coyote hunters can fire at close and distant targets. (Photo courtesy Jim Zumbo)

tions so quickly when running that it is almost unbelievable, and he has an instinct for picking the best possible escape route in a split second.

The bobcat lacks the keen nose and finely tuned senses of the coyote, but he remains one of the few predators we know little about.

End of the chase.

Index